P9-DNO-168

"TIMELESS . . . UNDENIABLY COMPELLING."
—*Redbook*

"How strange that this should be the club we belong to: women who have been to hell and back. But we all understand what this means. It's a membership badge we wear with knowing looks and lines on our foreheads. . . . Such has been our womanquest. The relationships, careers, children, dreams, betrayals, hopes, wins, losses . . . Our feelings have blended. Our stories converge."

So begins the extraordinary new book by one of today's most renowned and influential spiritual leaders. A hugely popular proponent and interpreter of *A Course in Miracles*, Marianne Williamson has made a phenomenal impact on audiences worldwide, via her captivating lectures and TV appearances.

With *A Woman's Worth*, Williamson turns her charismatic voice—and the same empowering, spiritually enlightening wisdom that energized her landmark work, *A Return to Love*—to exploring the crucial role of women in the world today. Drawing deeply and candidly on her own experiences, the author illuminates her thought-provoking positions on such issues as beauty and age, relationships and sex, children and careers, and the reassurance and reassertion of the feminine in a patriarchal society.

Cutting across class, race, religion, *and* gender, *A Woman's Worth* speaks powerfully and persuasively to a generation in need of healing, and in search of harmony.

Please turn the page for glowing reviews of
A Woman's Worth . . .

A
WOMAN'S
WORTH

❋

A Ballantine Book
Published by The Random House Publishing Group

Copyright © 1993 by Marianne Williamson

Published in the United States by Ballantine Books, an imprint of
The Random House Publishing Group, a division of Random House, Inc.,
New York, and simultaneously in Canada by Random House of Canada
Limited, Toronto.

www.ballantinebooks.com

This edition published by arrangement with Random House, Inc.

Library of Congress Catalog Card Number: 93-90550

ISBN 0-345-38657-4

Cover design by Ruth Ross

Cover art by Maxfield Parish,
Ecstasy (detail), 1929.
Courtesy Alma Gilbert Galleries, Burlingame, CA.

Manufactured in the United States of America

First Ballantine Books Edition: April 1994

35 34 33 32

A WOMAN'S WORTH

Marianne Williamson

THE RANDOM HOUSE PUBLISHING GROUP
New York

For
Sophie Ann, Jane, and Emma

PREFACE

When I told girlfriends I was writing a book about women, most of them said something like this: "For us, for women who have been to hell and back?"

How strange that this should be the club we belong to: women who have been to hell and back. But we all understand what that means. It's a membership badge we wear with knowing looks and lines on our foreheads. Most of us have known at least one divorce or one devastating breakup, whether we were married or not. Other circumstances can get us into the club as well: abortion, disease, a variety of public or private humiliations, drugs, alcohol, the death of a loved one, incompetent parents, sick children. It's everything we thought life would never be like. We don't feel self-pity so much as fear and deep grief.

Such has been our womanquest. It is conscious and disciplined, or unconscious and unbridled. Whether we've learned anything or not, our suffering has shaped who we are, and for better or for worse we've been changed by the past few years. We are not who we would have been had we not descended. We have a lot of stories and a lot to edit.

In writing this book, I have no purpose other than a creative spill of my own guts. But that in itself is a passionate purpose, and I have seen how like my guts are to those of other women. The relationships, careers, children, dreams, betrayals, hopes, wins, losses—all these form my landscape too. Our feelings have blended. Our stories converge.

Every writer hopes her words will open a door, will offer a passage of light the reader can glide through. I dare to dream that dream for this book.

Marianne Williamson
Los Angeles

CONTENTS

A
WOMAN'S
WORTH

✳

ONE

Glorious Queens and Slavegirls

The eternal feminine draws us upward.
—Johann Wolfgang von Goethe

It's very difficult being a woman. It's very difficult being a man too, I realize, but this is a book about women. Sam Keen wrote a book about men, which he called *Fire in the Belly*. My friend Tara called me up one day and told me she wanted to write a companion volume, *Volcano in the Uterus*. I laughed when she said that, but inside I was thinking, and *Catastrophes in the Breasts* and *Terror in the Ovaries* . . .

More women cry, loudly or silently, every fraction of every moment, in every town of every country, than anyone—man or woman—realizes. We cry for our children, our lovers, our parents, and ourselves.

We cry in shame because we feel no right to cry, and we cry in peace because we feel it's time we did cry. We cry in moans and we cry in great yelps. We cry for the world. Yet we think we cry alone.

We feel that no one hears. And we must all listen now. We must hold the crying woman's hand and minister to her tenderly, or she will turn—this collective feminine shadow self—into a monster who will go unheard no longer. This book is an effort to hear and understand her, in today's world, as she exists at this moment, imprisoned while still dressed in all her ancient, soiled regalia. She is like a child yet she is not a child. She is our mother, our daughter, our sister, our lover. She needs us now, and we need her.

WOMANHOOD TODAY is tentative and unsure, a thing defined more by what it isn't than by what it is. For some women, this is not a problem. They have risen above the complexities of society's projections and misunderstandings and now fly high above the clouds. For most women, however, the resistances they encountered as they reached for the sky were so great that their wings have now drooped, and they try no longer.

Womanhood is a mass pain of unspoken depth; and when we try to speak it, we're liable to be told, "There you go—complaining again!"

As long as this is true, not half but all of humanity is obstructed in its journey to our cosmic destination. This destination is far, far away, a place so deep inside us that we have barely glimpsed its outer walls.

This is a book about a woman's inner life. Here, we are our real selves, while in the outer world we are impostors. We're not sure why we're posing, except we have no clue how not to. We have forgotten the part we came here to play. We have lost the key to our own house. We're hanging out outside the door. The stress of being away so long from home is hurting us, even killing us. We must not stay away; we must find the key. For until we do, we will continue to shrivel—our faces, our breasts, our ovaries, our stories. We are drooping down and falling apart. If we knew how to moan, they would hear us on the moon.

But the dirt around us is moving, making room for tiny sprouts. Like every woman, I know what I know. Something is starting to happen. New things lie in store for the earth, and one of them is us. Womanhood is being recast, and we're pregnant, en masse, giving birth to our own redemption.

Watch. Wait. Time will unfold and fulfill its purpose. While we wait, we must not go unconscious. We must think and grow. Rejoice and dream, kneel and pray. There is holiness in the air today; modern priestesses are appearing all over. They are who we are, for they are us: friends, therapists, artists, businesswomen, teachers, healers, mothers. Start laughing, girls. We have a new calling.

You can tell who we are: We use whatever our business is as a front for talking about things that really matter. We're only stuck in this work, you see, because our real work was taken away from us several thousand years ago. We looked on the map, but our town was gone. We looked through the catalog but couldn't find the course we wanted. It's as if someone removed our chair but couldn't take away our longing to sit.

Together we embark on a quest for our own enchantment. It will take us to a place where what is feminine is sacred, as are a lot of other things as well. There we can become who we are meant to be and live the life we are meant to live. But we need to see the lay of the land, and we need to see clearly the way back home.

"What?" you say. "Me, enchanted?" Yes, I say, and don't act so surprised. You knew when you were little that you were born for something special and no matter what happened to you, that couldn't be erased. The magic could not be drained from your heart any more than Lady Macbeth could wash the guilt from her hands. Sorry to tell you, but you had it right years ago, and then you forgot. You were born with a mystical purpose. In reading this now, you might remember what it is.

There are women who are enchanted, living here now as there have always been and always will be. They are bearers of the Goddess's torch, however dim its light may shine. On the inner planes, they are priestesses and queens. They are absolutely powerful; they have made it past the gates. I have known a few, and I have heard of others. And I will tell you all I know, of who they are and how they do it.

• • •

AT EVERY MOMENT, a woman makes a choice: between the state of the queen and the state of the slavegirl. In our natural state, we are glorious beings. In the world of illusion, we are lost and imprisoned, slaves to our appetites and our will to false power. Our jailer is a three-headed monster: one head our past, one our insecurity, and one our popular culture.

Our past is a story existing only in our minds. Look, analyze, understand, and forgive. Then, as quickly as possible, chuck it.

Our insecurity is inevitable in the absence of personal meaning. Without a sense of connection to deeper, more noble ideas, we are doomed to a desperate struggle for things that fill us up: the job, the relationship, the looks, the body. We are tyrannized by a belief that we are inadequate. No nazi with machine gun could be a more tormenting presence.

The monster's third head is the pop culture we collectively spend billions of dollars supporting each year. It does not support us in return. Most movies do not love us, most advertising does not love us, most of the fashion industry does not love us, and most rock and roll does not love us (very sad that one—it used to). Like many battered wives, we look endlessly for love in places with no capacity to love us back. We must consciously choose to do this no longer.

Until we do, the monster will keep us locked up in his dungeon. Deep inside us, however, is an inborn escape hatch. It's a love that doesn't end or waver or make money off us or play games with us or stomp on our hearts. It's our spiritual core. Within it, we exist as cosmic royals: mothers, sisters, daughters of the sun and moon and stars. Within this realm, we find God, the Goddess, and our own sweet selves. Laugh at all of this at your emotional peril.

The outside world contains many vicious dreams, and those dreams have a hold on us. I know, I know. But I have heard some spiritual secrets, and so have you if your ears have been open. There are ways to transcend, ways to go forward. We can leave the monster behind. We can find deliverance for our hearts and come home to scented roses.

There is a door, a true one, a passage of emotional opportunity, and we are perfectly capable of sailing through it. Angels are holding it open for all of us. But you must be bold. Sissies can't see angels, so sissies can't find the door.

MOST WOMEN I KNOW are priestesses and healers, although many don't yet know it, and some never will. We are all of us sisters of a mysterious order.

Several years ago, I found myself waking up at four-fifteen each morning, my eyes popping open as if on cue. Later, I learned that in days of old four-fifteen was considered the witching hour. How perfect, that seemed to me. We would all awaken at the same time and join with one another, and worship, and know.

We still know things. As best we can, we continue to commune. "Is the baby asleep?" "Did you get the job?" "Did he come home?" "Does your pain feel better?" "Have you heard the news?" We begin as friends and then develop a shared realization, conscious or unconscious, that we are bearers of magic and that our circles of support are circles of mystical power. It's a woman's prerogative to know of magic, and to practice magic, and to use her knowledge to help the world.

We are used to thinking of Friday the thirteenth as bad luck. In fact, Friday the thirteenth was the day the witches gathered. When the patriarchal system, headed by the early church, began to squelch the power of women, witches were deemed evil, and many great women were deemed witches. Their meeting time, then, was seen as bad luck rather than as what it truly was: a time for women to gather and share energy and pray together and heal.

Our mystical power should not be relegated to the distant past. It still exists. I want mine now, and so does every woman I know. Our power is not evil but good. We must reclaim our goodness as well as our power. Today, the reason we haven't found our grail, the key to who we are as women, is because we look for it in worlds of false power, the very worlds that took it away from us in the first place. Neither men nor work can restore our lost scepter. Nothing in this world can take us home. Only the radar in our hearts can do that, and when it does, we return to our castles. There we are crowned in gold, and we remember how to laugh, how to love, how to rule.

We can't look to the world to restore our worth; we're here to restore our worth to the world. The world outside us can reflect our glory, but it cannot create it. It cannot crown us. Only God can crown us, and he already has.

I ONCE SAW a funny birthday card. On the front it read *Happy birthday to my daughter, the princess.* On the inside, it continued, *From your mother, the queen.*

What is a princess, and what is a queen? Why is *princess* often a pejorative description of a certain type of woman, and the word *queen* hardly ever applied to women at all? A princess is a girl who knows that she will get there, who is on her way perhaps but is not there yet. She has power but she does not yet wield it responsibly. She is indulgent and frivolous. She cries but not yet noble tears. She stomps her feet and does not know how to contain her pain or use it creatively.

A queen is wise. She has earned her serenity, not having had it bestowed on her but having passed her tests. She has suffered and grown more beautiful because of it. She has proven she can hold her kingdom together. She has become its vision. She cares deeply about something bigger than herself. She rules with authentic power.

Our kingdom is our life, and our life is our kingdom. We are all meant to rule from a glorious place. When God is on the throne, then so are we. When God is in exile, our lands are at war and our kingdoms are in chaos.

To be a princess is to play at life. To be a queen is to be a serious player. Audrey Hepburn was a queen, Barbara Jordan is a queen, Gloria Steinem is a queen, Judy Collins is a queen. Most of us are a little of both. The purpose of life as a woman is to ascend to the throne and rule with heart.

The growth of a girl into a woman, a princess into a queen, is not a liberal transition. Like any true creative flow, it is radical. That is not to say it is angry or harsh. But it is radical, the way truth is radical—and birth and art and real love and death. It changes things. It represents a shift in core beliefs, a belly-up of dominant paradigms. Without this shift, a woman seesaws between the brink of disaster and the brink of salvation. She goes from moments of bliss to moments of terror. And then the children, and the world, begin to seesaw with her.

When a woman has owned her passionate nature, allowing love to flood her heart, her thoughts grow wild and fierce and beautiful. Her juices flow. Her heart expands. She has thrown off crutch and compromise. She has glimpsed the enchanted kingdom, the vast and magical realms of the Goddess within her. Here, all things are transformed. And there is a purpose to this: that the world might be mothered back to a great and glorious state. When a woman conceives her true self, a miracle occurs and life around her begins again.

Mary's was a virgin birth, and the word *virgin* means "a woman unto herself." The actualized woman is powerful unto herself and gives birth to things divine. Today we have the chance to give birth to a healed and transformed world. This cannot be done without a major uprising of the glorious in women, because nothing can be healed without the female powers that nurture and protect, intuit and endure. What does this mean for the individual woman living day to day in a world that resists her expansion and makes her wrong for her passions? It means finding others who have seen the same light. They are everywhere, and like us they await instruction. They are men and women, young and old, who have heard the joke but take it too seriously to laugh. It is funny but also tragic, this cutting off at the pass of the life-force of half of humanity. Something new is brewing, and let's be grateful that it is. The Queen is coming to reclaim her girls.

When the Queen emerges, she is magical and enchanting. She is calm and happy. She creates order where there was none. She has grown new eyes.

When a woman rises up in glory, her energy is magnetic and her sense of possibility contagious. We have all seen glorious women, full of integrity and joy, aware of it, proud of it, overflowing with love. They shine. I have known this state in other women and, at moments, in myself. But it could be a stronger statement, a more collective beat. We don't have to do anything to be glorious; to be so is our nature. If we have read, studied, and loved; if we have thought as deeply as we could and felt as deeply as we could; if our bodies are instruments of love given and received—then we are the greatest blessing in the world. Nothing needs to be added to that to establish our worth.

Just stand there. Sit there. Smile. Bless. What a hunger is left unfulfilled in our society for no reason other than that women have been so devalued by others and so dishonored by ourselves.

EVERY WOMAN I KNOW wants to be a glorious queen, but that option was hardly on the multiple-choice questionnaire we were handed when we were little girls. Rarely did anyone tell us we could choose to be magic.

When I was a child, there was a woman who lived across the street named Betty Lynn. She was sort of a cross between Auntie Mame and Jayne Mansfield. I thought she was the most beautiful, most fascinating, most wonderful woman in the world. Betty Lynn was wild and gorgeous and drove a Cadillac. I thought it was beige, but she called it the color of champagne. She wanted a thatched roof on her guest house. She obviously had sex with her husband. She always told me I was wonderful.

Years later, I remembered the scotch and water that was usually in her hand, and many things began to make sense that hadn't made sense when I was young. But at the time, she was a model of sorts, a glamorous woman who made me see magic when all I found on my side of the street was a lid placed on my emotions and disapproval of my more outrageous passions.

Why, in the thirty-odd years since I knew this woman, have I never forgotten her? What did she represent that struck me as so real, so passionate, so enchanted?

Whatever it was, the alcohol helped her let it out, but then the alcohol enslaved her, and then it killed her. That's clear. But why do people who have the most ardor, the most enchantment, the most power so often feel the need for drugs and alcohol? They do not drink just to dull their pain; they drink to dull their ecstasy. Betty Lynn lived in a world that doesn't know from ecstatic women, or want to know, or even allow them to exist. In former times, she would have had her own temple, and people from all around would have gathered to sit at her feet and hear her pronounce them marvelous. She would have mixed herbs and oils. But an unenlightened world began to burn these women, and the world burns them still. Betty Lynn crucified herself before anyone else had a chance to. Many of us are a little like her, choosing to implode rather than take on society's punishment. Those of us who don't must bear society's wrath. But we live through it, bruised and battered though we might be. And more and more of us are now living to tell the tale, surviving the fire, surviving sober, and, hopefully, altered in such a way that our daughters will have an easier time.

WE HAVE A JOB TO DO, reclaimimg our glory. It's work, and it will not please everyone. We will be called grandiose. We will be accused of being in dangerous denial, of our faults, our neuroses, our weaknesses. But it's an ancient trick this, telling a woman that her glory is her sickness. You bet we're in denial. We deny the power of weakness to hold us back, be it the weakness of the world or the weakness in our own past. We are on to better things, such as owning our beauty and honoring the courage it has taken us to get here and claiming our natural power to heal and be healed. We're not grandiose, but we're tired—tired of pretending we are guilty when we know we're innocent, that we're plain when we know we're beautiful, and that we're weak when we know we're strong. For far too long, we have forgotten we are cosmic royals. Our mothers forgot, their mothers forgot, and their mothers before them. We regret their tears; we mourn their sadness. But now, at last, we break the chain.

When the Goddess is ready to reemerge, she reemerges. There is no person or law or institution that can hold her back. Like the energy of Christ, of which she is a part, the Goddess finds her way into the hearts and minds of millions of individual women, and they change. It doesn't matter who doesn't change when enough people do. This is true in any social, political, or cultural tide. When an idea reaches critical mass, there is no stopping the shift its presence induces.

One of the most sophisticated, insidious conspiracies has been perpetrated against women. Thousands of years of history have been largely rewritten in order to erase from collective memory the fact that men were not always on top. Archaeological evidence now argues for the existence of a twenty-thousand-year period of history when men and women lived as equals, with neither sex dominating the other. The earth flourished. The so-called feminine qualities of compassion, nurturing, and nonviolence were shared by men and women alike and were the most vital elements of social structure. Women were revered as priestesses and healers. Our intuitive strengths were not scorned but respected. Our more fluid modes of thought and feeling were seen as creative rhythms, not flaky girl stuff. To our mates and lovers, our children and friends, we were natural priestesses. We healed one another through our compassionate connection to spirit and earth. But we took a detour, and the Goddess was masked.

The world is currently set up according to masculine models of thought and structure, and it has been for thousands of years. Aggression, force, domination, and control have been at the heart of our social agreements. Organization, technology, and rational analysis have been the order of this very long day. During this time, the feminine principles of nonviolence and surrender and the values of intuition, nurturing, and healing were pushed aside. We forgot the power of a tender touch. Slowly but surely, generation after generation, over thousands of years, the feminine was made to seem ridiculous. She was debased in men as well as in women, all of us risking shame when choosing to relate to her. We could know her in bed, and she was good with children. But other than that, she didn't belong here. She wasn't silenced, just invalidated. She could still speak, but she wouldn't be heard.

Note the Statue of Liberty and Emma Lazarus's poem inscribed at its base. "Give me your tired, your poor," Liberty says, "Your huddled masses yearning to breathe free." Her manifesto of concern for human life became a cornerstone of compassionate strength at the center of American consciousness. But our national mind, dissociated from its feminine nature, has sought domination and control instead of sharing and nurturing. Our words began to change from "give me your tired" to "tell them to go home." We kept the statue, but we no longer take her seriously. During the 1986 centennial celebration in New York Harbor, I was struck by the irony of the spectacular party thrown at the Statue of Liberty. A government that had systematically dismantled the elements of the social and political policy that formed the lifeblood of Emma Lazarus's poem now hosted a lavish celebration at Liberty's feet. We treat her the way we treat all women during times when the Goddess is silenced: We dress her up and show her off, but we don't want to listen to what she has to say.

And no one will listen to us until we listen to ourselves. The Goddess awakens in our hearts before she awakens in the world. We must notice that she exists. We must honor and worship and revere her, regardless of the name by which we call her. For not to do so is to dishonor ourselves. She is our feminine essence. She is the female power and the spiritual glory that lies within every woman and every man.

FORGET LOOKING for earthly role models, because there aren't many; and even when we find them, they live their own lives and not ours. We must look instead inside ourselves. The Goddess doesn't enter us from outside; she emerges from deep within. She is not held back by what happened to us in the past. She is conceived in consciousness, born in love, and nurtured by higher thinking. She is integrity and value, created and sustained by the hard work of personal growth and the discipline of a life lived actively in hope.

Build community. Nurture those less fortunate. Become yourself. Seek God. No less potent steps than these will be deep enough to move you forward.

The crucifixion of the Goddess—the invalidation of feminine beliefs and values—lies at the heart of all our painful dramas. But crucifixion is merely a prelude to resurrection, and we are now living at the beginning stages of the resurrection of the Goddess. This occurs not through the reemergence of any one particular symbol, be it Mary, Quanyin, Gaea, or Isis. She has many names and faces, but her most important one is your own. Her reemergence now is a cellular upheaval, a rising up from the depths of individual women throughout the world. It is a new spirit, a new strength, a new conviction, and a new care. The most glorious angels light up the sky when the Queen

of heaven returns to her throne. These are arche-
typal images that trace for us the trail of the feminine
journey, its purpose and direction. Women must remember how important it is to honor women. In
"reforming" the Christian church, Martin Luther
chose to throw out Mary. In rediscovering the church
within us, we choose to bring her back.

A powerful tool for the reclamation of our glorious
feminine identity is the worship of female gods. As the
mother of the son of God, the Virgin Mary gave
human birth to God's expression on earth. Without
her body and her nurturing, the Word would have
remained just a word. Through her womb and her
maternal compassion, she became the vehicle through
which the Word was made flesh.

Mary is real. She is a symbol, but she is also much
more than that. She is an energy, an essential hierarchi-
cal truth or being, that is the essence of all women. She
is found in many religions. Some call her the Goddess.
She is active psychically, participating alchemically in
the areas of our suffering and our liberation. For millions of people, she is no joke.

At her birth, her parents knew her life was to be
used in the service of a great and holy cause. She was
raised to be a channel of light, which is to say she was
guided in the direction of her highest human qualities.
She was entrusted by God with a profound and
mighty task on earth, and over the years her body,
soul, and mind were prepared for that service.

To think of ourselves in terms of Mary's purpose

and ministry is to heal our wounds. It is to fill our minds with the light that casts out the darkness of myriad neuroses. In every area of our experience as women, we are lost and disconnected because we do not perceive ourselves in spiritual terms. We think of ourselves as flesh and bone, résumés and relationships, clothes and cosmetics. The truth of who we are, why we're here, and where we're going is far more spectacular than any of these worldly things indicate. We are God's precious vessels, and we are always pregnant with his possibilities.

This is not the kind of knowledge that sounds sane when divulged at a cocktail party. But in private, in meditation, in churches, mosques, and synagogues, at ashrams, and in support groups, it is the stuff of truth that sets us free. And women need desperately to be set free. We have been enslaved for centuries by our ignorance and deep forgetfulness. It is time to remember we're the daughters of God.

One of the themes of healing in the nineties is deeper spiritual practice. When I say, "Go talk to Mary," I *mean* "Go talk to Mary"—as in, go to a church, light a candle, sit in a pew, and let yourself become very serious about this. Tell her, "Mary, I wish to know who I am as a wife or girlfriend or mother or daughter. I wish to be the woman I am capable of being. I wish to have your purity and clarity and level of enlightenment. May the essence of my womanhood become more radiant than my external self." And that's it. It doesn't matter what your religion is. Talking to Mary doesn't make you a Catholic, nor does being a Catholic give you a special "in." If Mary doesn't feel comfortable for you, that's OK too. Find a Greek goddess or a female Indian avatar you can relate to, or any other symbol of feminine divinity, and begin a relationship with her.

Don't see this as a joke or treat it as a toy. The world as it is has very little use for your womanhood. You are considered a weaker sex and are treated as a sexual object. You are thoroughly dispensable except for bearing children. Your youth is the measure of your worth, and your age is the measure of your worthlessness. Do not look to the world for your sustenance or for your identity as a woman because you will not find them there. The world despises you. God adores you.

TWO

※

Internal Light

> i found god in myself
> & i loved her
> i loved her fiercely.
>
> —Ntozake Shange

I looked at a picture of my face today. I hated the picture because it doesn't say who I am. But then, most women's faces don't tell the truth. Or, I should say, most women's hairdos don't tell the truth; their clothes don't tell the truth; their jewelry doesn't tell the truth. There are what appear to be magnificent exceptions; but far too often when their adornments tell a great story, the women themselves don't. Most of us—most American women—are completely bewildered by our hair, clothes, and makeup. That's why we spend so much money on them. We're looking for help.

The next time you meet another woman at a party,

assume she experienced at least 10 percent as much angst over what to wear that night as you did. Multiply that angst by the number of women in America who went out to dinner that night. Now add up the stress.

Feminine beauty is not a function of clothes or hair or makeup, although billions of dollars are spent in this country each year by women who have been convinced by the advertising industry that it is. Beauty is an internal light, a spiritual radiance that all women have but which most women hide, unconsciously denying its existence. What we do not claim remains invisible. This is why the process of personal transformation—the true work of spiritual growth, whether couched in religious terms or not—is the only antidote to the pernicious effects of society's backlash against genuine female empowerment. Society programs us, through the subliminal messages of popular culture, to believe that we're not truly desirable as women unless we adhere to the current standards of physical beauty. The reason we're such fertile ground for the dark forces of such lies and social manipulation is that we're dissociated from the genuine light of self-awareness.

The woman who is truly self-aware knows that her self is a light from beyond this world, a spiritual essence that has nothing to do with the physical world. Those of us who strongly believe in the reality of spirit are quickly invalidated by a worldly power system that senses within spiritual truth the seeds of its own destruction. For if we truly believed in an internal light, we would not believe in the power of external forces, and we would not be so easy to dominate and control. We would not be tempted to see hair and clothes and makeup as sources of so much of our self-esteem and the ideal beauty of a fashion model as a sign that we are not beautiful at all. In the words of Naomi Wolf, "We as women are trained to see ourselves as cheap imitations of fashion photographs, rather than seeing fashion photographs as cheap imitations of women."

But we are ultimately responsible for how we see ourselves, regardless of the horrible images of women—pornographic, misogynistic, and violent— that permeate our culture. Much of traditional religious imagery has represented women as inferior, even evil. It is only an enlightened spiritual worldview that reveals both men and women in all our true glory. We are glorious because we are not beings of this world at all. Our spiritual essence is nonmaterial, nonphysical; and when we become aware of this, we are genuinely empowered. The more we develop what is called in Alcoholics Anonymous our "conscious contact" with truth as God created it, the less we are prey to the lies of a fearful world. When we are truly aware of our spiritual glory, a varicose vein or two is not that big a deal.

A WOMAN ONCE STOOD in line in front of me at a 7-Eleven. She was fat, at least fifty pounds overweight. Her hair was bleached blond. She was buying copies of the *Globe* and the *National Enquirer*, a bag of peanuts, and a huge prepackaged cookie. I felt her misery.

I said a little prayer for her. I've been as bummed out as she was, although I haven't acted out my despair in quite the same ways. I've known, as we all have, her desire to escape into a world where she wouldn't have to face the harshness of another day like this one.

At the same time, I know she cares desperately, because we all do. Her body says she doesn't care, her hair says she doesn't care, and her choice of reading matter says she doesn't care. But she does care. And if she felt she had a choice, she would open wide and act like a queen. But she doesn't realize she has the option. She thinks that only queens get to be queens. She doesn't know that every woman who is a queen simply knew she could be one, and everyone else is still pretending she can't. That's all that separates the queens from the slavegirls: a shift in consciousness from denial to acceptance of personal power.

That woman's education may have been poor, and her family dysfunctional, and her present circumstances somewhere between horrible and catastrophic. But she remains a potential queen. A change in consciousness produces miracles. The growth of a woman from slavegirl to queen is the miracle of feminine transformation. It begins with a decision to change and a willingness to accept God's help.

If by any chance the woman I saw at the 7-Eleven is reading this book, say this prayer if you wish to: Dear God, I am willing to relinquish my life of limitation and despair. I invite your spirit to renew my life. Amen. It is God's will that we be beautiful, that we love and be loved and prosper in all good things. It is God's will that we all become the goddesses we were created to be.

EVEN WHEN A WOMAN has been blessed with great abundance, she often has a difficult time allowing herself to receive it all. I have a friend who has a wonderful life. She lives half the year in Europe and flies in her own private plane back and forth between her various houses around the world. She has a husband who is perfect for her. She has a successful, fulfilling career in fashion design and two happy, healthy children. What she doesn't have is a thin waist.

Her suffering over her weight casts a giant shadow over a life that is otherwise so sweet. She has tried every diet, every doctor, every technique she could find to help herself lose the excess pounds and keep them off. What she had not tried, until recently, was confronting whatever it was in her that had so much invested in being fat.

There is no diet or doctor that can prevail against a strongly held belief. In the case of my friend, and in the case of many people who carry around one thing, whatever it is, that blocks them from total joy, that belief is this: If I am too happy, too successful, too perfect, *I will not be loved.* There has to be something that lets other people know that I'm really "one of them," that I'm miserable too. I'm really not taking away their piece of the pie. I'm really not perfect, so they don't have to hate me.

For some women, it's weight; for others it's something else we do or think or say to make it appear that we're having a hard time too. We're unconsciously afraid of a reaction against us if we dare to shine fully, embrace joy, and permit ourselves to have too great a life. The injunction against winning is subtle but strong, so we ourselves make sure no one will be able to accuse us of having broken the great unspoken rule: Do not experience heaven on earth. The punishment can be severe, at least emotionally, for those of us who break the rule. From friends to family to people who don't even know us, the chorus of disapproval can ring loudly against women who dare to break through the ultimate glass ceiling.

What is the antidote to such a threat, whether it comes from others or is in our own minds? It is to realize that it is God's will that each of us, every woman, man, and child, be happy, whole, and successful. It is impossible to overestimate the psychic damage done by the delusions, pseudoreligious and other, that God is somehow happier or we are somehow purer if we are suffering just a bit. The truth is not that God is happier or that we are better, but that the institutions that told us so are happier, because suffering keeps us in our place, where we are easier to control.

But how can there be a joyful planet without its being inhabited by joyful people? Our embrace of joy doesn't rob others of the possibility. Quite the opposite is true—it liberates them, if they choose to be liberated. If I see before me a person who lives a truly happy life, I can follow my ego or follow my heart. My ego will try to argue that the person must be guilty of *something*, but my heart will recognize that his or her success is *my* success, if I can allow myself to applaud instead of criticize and bless instead of condemn.

When I first began my career as a lecturer, doing my best to make a positive difference in my community, I often heard people say, "Isn't she nice!" But as my work became visible to a larger public, the same work done the same way and with, if anything, even greater dedication, drew cries of "Who does she think she is?" I have never received the criticism for failure that I have for success, and it is clear to me that people in our society at least unconsciously hold the conviction that someone else's success limits their own, makes them lesser, and puts a permanent lid on their own chances. The world believes in finite resources and in everybody's guilt. As long as we adhere to these pernicious beliefs, we will not only fail to let others shine, but we will never be able to allow ourselves to shine fully either.

And if we, like my friend, stand in fear of what fear says, in the minds of others or in our own minds, we then conspire in a thought system that cruelly limits us and our daughters and their daughters too. We refuse to allow ourselves to help the world as much as we might were we to allow ourselves to be all that we can be. God gives us abundance in all things that we might use it in behalf of the healing of the world. If we forge ahead and continue to embrace the life that God has opened up for us, then we will break through the cloud banks of other people's disapproval, whether real or imagined. When we ourselves no longer feel guilty, when we have liberated ourselves from the limited thinking of a society deeply afraid of ecstatic women, then we will no longer encounter people who attack us. Or if we do, we will no longer care. And having broken through the clouds, we will see a new light and meet new friends.

Don't stop now. Keep going. The next time someone makes you feel as though, winning as you are, perhaps you're getting too big for your britches, say to them silently, "I haven't even started yet."

WE EXIST IN GOD'S MIND as total and complete beings: There is nothing Madison Avenue can give us that will make us more beautiful women. We are beautiful because God created us that way. Some of us know of our beauty and express it and celebrate it. But beauty itself is not given to us by anyone; it is a power we have within us from the gate, a radiance inside us. I have known women who were not physically beautiful but who expressed themselves so magnificently that the result was a beautiful woman. I have known other women who were practically perfect physical specimens but were so unaware of their own light that the effect of their beauty was nil.

What should women do with a fractured sense of self? Many of us are good at describing and analyzing our insecurities; what we must do now is invoke the healed self. Within each one of us, in the realm of pure awareness, is the Goddess, the glorious female, the cosmic queen.

If you're a sensitive creature, and almost every woman is, then your heart is open to all things. Every cry we recognize. Every tear we relate to. Every sigh contains our own. And we are stymied by this, immobilized until we make a run in the other direction. A woman's emotional instrumentation, more delicate and intricate than any computer chip from Japan, is as fragile as it is powerful. It turns against us when it is not used for healing, constructive purposes. It is as if God has said, "Here. Feel this," and we don't know whether he said that because he is angry at us or because he loves us.

Without a potent inner life, a spiritual connection, a woman tosses on a storm of hysterical emotions. Like a beautiful vase into which an ocean is poured, shattering the glass because the container cannot accommodate the force or the volume, we are ill prepared for the powerful and dynamic energies that race through our veins.

We remember everything. We remember Mary holding the baby. We remember watching him die. We remember wars and murders we don't even know we remember. We remember ancient temple sites, healings and prophesies. We remember genital mutilation and Sophie's choice. We were present at the beginning of things; and if people would only let us, we would teach the marvelous lessons we learned from the experience. We cannot get to our knowledge because the world is too loud. And we tend to make it louder as we cry out in pain, pretending we are singing. We add to the world's cacophony because we don't know it's our job to turn down the noise and listen to silent symphonies. No one told us that. For thousands of years, they haven't wanted us to know. But when we break free and see the game for what it is, we will let out a howl, and our silence will be deafening. We will hear the holy choir of angels, our eyes will brighten, and our smiles will burst forth. We will see the angels and know the angels, and do lunch with them, and speak their case. We will be intimate with the stars and ride rainbows to ancient Greece. We will light up like lamps, and the world will never be the same again.

The men around us need this change as much as we do and maybe more. Our children see in us the truth we do not see: that we have power unmatched by any other creature. When we remember our royal inheritance, men will become our true partners, our kings. We have all been crowned, and yet the throne awaits us. Now is the time to reclaim our title, to bow our heads before God and receive, in awareness, our conscious coronation. When we do, the world will change quickly.

It will change when every woman gets it that we are all beautiful, powerful, and strong. That we deserve love and approval and support. That we would all be glorious if we could only spread our wings. That we are, each one of us, a portion of a great and mighty Goddess self. What a light will arise from behind the mountains on the morning of our remembrance. What a sun will shine through the fog of tears when we embrace our true selves at last.

Until we do, we will remain sad. Our imprisonment has been long and cruel. We have dressed to hide ourselves and spoken to misrepresent ourselves, and worked to change ourselves. We have imagined our passions to be wrong and our instincts out of line. We have suffered a wounding, but a miracle has occurred. There is a Woman in the Sky, and she has come to take us home.

The Woman in the Sky has long, beautiful hair and skin that glows. She smiles from a place deeper than the center of the earth. She has a beautiful speaking voice, and she can sing. She has mothered us all. We have inherited her gifts and her healing powers. In ancient agreement, we have come to this point to remember her together. Like a volcano erupting after years of stillness, we now explode with heat and power and liquid strength.

The Woman in the Sky has entered into us. Like every aspect of the cosmic energy of which she is a part, she permeates the cells of those who have invited her in. She gives us new life, that we might give it to others. Through her power within us, we redeem all things. For centuries, we have been ripped apart inside, our personalities disconnected from our most crucial knowledge. We have been concerned with small things when we ourselves are huge. Those days are over. We must begin again.

We begin with a promise, made to ourselves and to each other, that we will never go back. We will never again fail to realize how hard it is for every woman, as it has been for us, to face the challenges and resistances of a world that treats women as second-class citizens. We have been relegated to such a position not because we are less intelligent. The world treats us as second-class citizens as a means of control over us—as if were we simply named weak, then we would be weak. And we have fallen for that ruse. We have been defeated by the power inherent in naming things. The spell that this power has cast on us must now be broken. We must name ourselves queens.

Patriarchal power has resisted our strength, but the oppressive forces of an entire kingdom—and the thought and treatment of women as inferior *are* a mental kingdom—have no power in the face of a woman who knows she is a queen. The negative ego fears women not because we are weak but because we are so powerful, and because our power comes from an invisible realm. The rational mind can neither explain it nor control it, and to the negative ego this is unforgivable power.

Still, we must claim our mystical forces. We must forge ahead, through the dark and prickly forces of ridicule and resistance in whatever form they take, doing what we came here to do and being who we came here to be. Oppression of women is far from over, and often women themselves are the ones who make the world even harder for other women. But this phenomenon will fade away as female-oppressing females become healed of their own self-hatred. On the other side of this jungle is a new and glorious day on earth, when our daughters will not be judged wrong for their passions or held back because they are bursting with such power, strength, and love.

Children help. Sunsets help. Good men help. The beach helps. Reading about women who have been great in their field helps. Meditation helps. Prayer helps.

DON'T YOU LOVE IT when some incredibly beautiful woman like Linda Evans or Cindy Crawford tells us that the real beauty secret is finding your inner light? Right. But I've done the same things these women have done to find my inner light, and while it's true I'm happier, I still don't look like them. The point is I never will, but I look the way I look, and how I look shouldn't be such an awfully big deal. It isn't for men, and it shouldn't be for us. It would behoove Americans to recognize that in other cultures the range of what is considered beautiful is much wider than it is in ours, as is the age range that defines physical beauty.

In many ways, I used to try to be a certain way for men: my personality, my looks, my behavior. I still try to improve myself in those areas, but I do so for myself, for my own joy. To please a man can be exciting, but to try to be a certain way for him, to try to create ourselves instead of revealing ourselves, is to come from such a lack of self-esteem that it would be hard to keep a man interested anyway.

And who knows how we are supposed to be? I can't figure it out, and at times I've tried. But I do know this: On the days when I feel love and compassion and forgiveness in my life, I'm happier and more attractive to other people. Those feelings are the mystical keys to beauty and happiness. It is so simple, and it doesn't cost a thing. From pseudosophisticated corners, there is resistance to such an easy message. For if women were really to believe these things—that love in our hearts could renew our lives—billions of dollars would be spent elsewhere.

And why are we always trying to figure out how to be more attractive to men, anyway? Why shouldn't they work a little and try to figure out how to be attractive to us? Not every man knows how to handle a woman who is full of passion, glory, power, and intelligence. So what should we do? Shrink? Many, many women do. And then perhaps they're married or hitched. But they're not necessarily happy, and neither are their men. It is better to be alone than to be living at half throttle.

Men in our culture have been spoiled, treated with false reverence instead of respect. We have enabled them to think a woman is just a body, a clotheshorse, and a sex machine, and we have done so by acting at times as if we were those things. A woman is an ever-deepening mystery that takes years and humility and great patience to fathom. Having become blind to this fact ourselves, we have over and over and over again put up with the most irreverent attitudes. We have failed to teach our sons, much less our daughters, what a magnificent thing a woman is.

Break the chain. Don't let another woman inherit your last spoiled-brat lover like a pair of uncomfortable shoes you took back to the store. If he doesn't get it, let him know. Walk on by. We have spent enough time in the heart of darkness; now we are headed for the heart of light.

THREE

A Magnificent Adventure

In youth we learn; in age we understand.
—Marie von Ebner-Eschenbach

There is a collective force rising up on the earth today, an energy of the reborn feminine. She is peeking around corners, taking over businesses, tucking in the children, and making men go wild in every way. She knows us at our source. She is not, as we are not, lacking in virtue. She remembers our function on earth: that we should love one another. She has come to reclaim us. She has come to take us home.

As the feminine spirit seeks to rise, there are numerous forces seeking to push her back down. This is a time of a monumental shift, from the male dominance of human consciousness back to a balanced relationship between masculine and feminine. The Goddess archetype doesn't replace God; she merely keeps him company. She expresses his feminine face.

The resistance to this is stronger than most people know. The invalidation, the crucifixion, of feminine power is one of the most emotionally violent and subversive forces at work today. Time after time, the Goddess has been beaten, thwarted, shut down—emotionally, physically, politically, and socially—by men and women alike. Every time a woman is raped or beaten, every time a woman is attacked on the street or crucified in the press for no other reason than that she is a woman, every time a strong woman is squeezed out of the workplace because her presence there is threatening to the old order—we are witnessing the skirmishes of a vast invisible war. The fate of every woman alive today, whether she likes it or not, is that the story of her life shall be played out against this panorama. Her relationships with everyone and everything—from her parents to her teachers to her lovers to her children to her friends to her job to her employers to her employees to her community to her culture—have been, are, and will be affected by this gigantic conflagration.

We have no choice as to whether or not this is happening. Our only choice is whether we shall open our eyes. When we remain ignorant of the forces swirling around us, we suffer the consequences of all unconsciousness, remaining at the effect of forces over which we seem to have no control. Should we awaken to the truth of the moment, we can consciously usher in one of the most important human breakthroughs in history. We have the opportunity to forge a marriage between masculine and feminine, more potent and more vibrant than any we have experienced on the earth for ages—more beautiful, perhaps, than any the earth has ever known.

The story doesn't begin with grown women being massacred in the workplace or in the press. It begins with innocent little girls who become convinced, for whatever reason, that the *girl* within them isn't good enough. From there, they turn into women who are always seeking to deny their femininity. From there, they attract others who will want to do the same. In order to dismantle a social disorder in which women are oppressed, we must begin where it all started: a long, long time ago, when we were very, very young.

Many of us grew up in dysfunctional families, because modern society is a dysfunctional place. But the spiritual journey, the path of recovery and personal growth, is a detoxification process in which we bring up and out the negative beliefs we have carried with us from the past and which now poison the present. We then learn to invoke the flame within us, which did not go out during our dark and difficult years. However confused we might have become, angels protected and shielded us. Our spirits did not die. There is an ever-renewable natural strength within us that still exists and is accessible now, regardless of what Mommy did or didn't do, how Daddy loved us or ignored us, or whether we feel we've succeeded or failed at life so far. I call that innocent place within every woman the lost girl.

"I could have been a mystical princess! I *should* have been a mystical princess! I was *supposed* to be a mystical princess!" Thus cries the woman who has tried to reclaim her lost girl. The lost girl is still within us—the girl who wasn't allowed to blossom, the girl whose natural childhood instincts were unnaturally capped at puberty, the girl who was squelched in fear of the woman she would become. For years, we live damaged, cut off from the true expression of who we are because we don't *know* who we are. We are numb to our own creative juices. No one held a space for our gorgeousness, and now we can't find it. As maidens, we were crushed. We were treated with suspicious looks at the very moment someone should have been turning up the applause. We don't know how to be women because we were taught it was not OK to be girls. Our most natural impulses were thwarted and distorted. We were like lava channeled into plastic molds.

RECENTLY, I MET a woman in her early twenties who was deeply depressed. Looking at her, I saw myself fifteen or twenty years ago. I recognized every desperate feeling, every horrified thought. I asked her why she felt so sad. She told me she felt misunderstood by her father, who didn't want to pay for her therapy or for her to move to another city. She said she was trying to make her way in the world but kept falling down. She couldn't stay with any career for very long; she felt fat; she felt inadequate; she felt embarrassed and kept thinking that other people were laughing at her.

The reality, in this instance, is that of an exquisitely beautiful young woman, as fat as the pope is Jewish and as lacking in brains as Susan Sontag. Here is a girl who doesn't know how to find her glory.

But that's what our twenties are for, I told her. They are the time when the maiden turns into a woman, the princess becomes a queen, the child grows up. They are not the time to concentrate on our parents so much as they are the time to concentrate on ourselves and our own abilities. Her father's money came with a very high price tag, as it usually does. What she wanted in a protector was not to be found in Daddy but in God. The peace and security she was looking for could be found only within herself, through a search for a higher, more noble life, and an embrace of the glory within her.

I told her that a career grows out of who we are; who we are doesn't grow out of a career. Her goal must not be to find a job but to become a magnificent woman. That is the mystical calling of every woman's heart, and it is our core task as we grow up. Later on in life, we are often bound by things, by responsibilities, by people, and situations that keep us tied to certain spaces and times. But a young woman must fly free, away from Mommy and Daddy, away from the dense conventions of the world, away from childhood and into the arms of the Goddess, who awaits her. A hysterical depression can then become a magnificent adventure.

When I myself was about her age, I worked for a man who was, and still is, a master at logos. His intellect is staggering. At the time I knew him, I was a maiden, a young woman like my friend, whose thoughts were scattered like wind through a half-built house. I knew many things that I could not yet articulate. I felt different from others, unable to play the parts assigned to me by the world in which I lived. As for the man, I knew he couldn't truly see me. But still I felt that one day my life would turn out fine, and I knew he would be surprised when it did.

Everything he spoke of was factual; everything could be measured and proved by the scientific mind. I, with my feelings bruised and scorched, knew that the lessons I was learning were not from the intellect but from the trials of my heart. I knew these lessons had more to do with where the world was going than did any of his facts or figures. The heart would be the language of tomorrow because the heart is where our pain is.

Recently, I read that he had said of me, "She was the last person in the world you would have ever expected to be a success." I laughed when I read that. I understood his thinking. The feminine way seems weak to the masculine prejudice; and when I worked for him, I was a developing feminine spirit. Lots of tears, lots of drama. For thousands of years, the woman's way, our way, has been kept underground. Unlike Mary, we are not prepared for our role. No gracious, institutionalized structure is unrolled like a red carpet to usher us into our glory. We come into it covered in mess from our rocky ascent.

But now the Goddess is returning—she is making her way up—and people without eyes to see will be completely in the dark about the journey of women all around them. As the Goddess begins to make her claim on them, there will be more, rather than fewer, girls who appear to make no sense. The Goddess makes a dramatic entry. When a system is flooded with new and radical impressions, it seems to implode before making a quantum leap forward into something different. Thus, there are millions of girls who are depressed to a degree beyond what their families and friends find normal, but who are actually undergoing the feminine journey into full and actualized consciousness. One day they will be queens, and the transition wouldn't have happened had they not cracked up when they did.

THE PRINCESS DOES become a queen if she stays the road. It is as if there were a beautiful enchantress in a luminous bubble. She stands before us and beckons for us to become her. Faith in her invokes our best. We change. We become unlike who we used to be. It is the miracle we sensed when we were little girls: that one day we would live lives of joy in enchanted castles.

Let us seek all that is true and loving and good about

womanhood and ask for the blessings thereof, for ourselves and others. We ask that our womanhood bless
our communities, our families, our friends. We ask for
wisdom and guidance that we might reach the highest
vibration of humanity of which we are capable. We
look to God and his many teachers, to the Goddess
and her many faces, to show us what we do not know.
From here we grow, more each passing day, into the
women God would have us be. There is no higher
prayer. From there we shall know joy, and this is what
we were born for.

Joy is our goal, our destiny. We cannot know who
we are except in joy. Not knowing joy, we do not
know ourselves. When we are without joy, we grope
in the dark. When we are centered in joy, we attain
our wisdom. A joyful woman, by merely being, says it
all. The world is terrified of joyful women. Make a
stand. Be one anyway.

Joy is what happens when we allow ourselves to
recognize how good things are. Joy is not necessarily
what happens when things unfold according to our
own plans. How often that's happened—we married
the right man, had the children, got the job—and
we've still known despair. Joy is what happens when
we see that God's plan is perfect and we're already
starring in a perfect show. It demands that we have the
audacity to embrace the knowledge of just how beautiful we really are and how infinitely powerful we are
right now—without changing a thing—through the
grace that's consistently born and reborn within us.

Such an embrace is not arrogant but humble; it is not crazy but realistic. It is an appraisal of our lives through the eyes the Goddess gives us. I have not known a lot of joy, but I have known some. When I am there, in that golden circle where everything feels wonderful for no apparent reason, I try to memorize the feeling, the terrain, the scenery. I have noticed how full I feel at those moments, with an overwhelming sense of rightness about all things. I know that this is our natural state and that the purpose of our lives is to achieve it consistently.

For now, joy is a gift, an act of grace that's here when it's here and not when it's not. But perhaps joy can be practiced. Perhaps we can decide to be happy, to give joy before waiting to receive it. This is not denial but affirmation of the power inside us. Embracing joy heals depression. Then we become the ones who teach the meaning of joy to our children, as well as allowing them to teach it to us. We bring joy to one another, to men, to children, to God. Just knowing we're meant to do this increases its presence within us. Our deciding to be joyful demonstrates our willingness to relinquish the petty and negative preoccupations that stand in its way. When we give these up, a more joyful life has a chance to emerge. The Goddess doesn't fight our pain; when she is in our hearts, the pain is gone.

I THINK WOMEN can have it all, but not immediately. The various forces of our power take years to develop fully. One of the ideas we must agree on and continue to forge with individual and collective vigor is that a woman's life goes uphill at forty. The French say that a woman blossoms at forty, but in America we're still burdened by our abhorrence of age, particularly in women. I remember when I was younger and looked great in a way that only the young can look. But I'm also sure that in those days I had no clue as to what makes a woman glorious. Some young women do, I realize. They know much more than I did. But women my age and older who didn't know until now should continue to blossom as long as we're breathing. For me and for many other women forty and over, the pieces of the puzzle have only just begun to fit together.

What mature women want is this: the lightheartedness of our youth with the added depth our suffering of the past few years has given us. Through the grace of the Goddess, it is within our grasp to have both. Genuine spiritual experience transforms our suffering into something beautiful and lifts the heavy burdens from our hearts. The older we get, the lighter we can become. It takes effort to move in this direction, because it is counter to the ways of the world, but running counter to the ways of the world is the purpose of our lives.

The enlightened system isn't set up so that we work hard, finally find joy, experience it for a relatively short time, and then grow old and die. Unless we strive for an expanded, more compassionate vision of age and aging, the achievements we seek here are at best cruel mockeries of our pain-filled efforts.

Let us imagine a woman's life improving as she ages. Age doesn't have to be bad. It could, in fact, be magnificent, if we would take our spiritual lives more seriously. Throughout our twenties and thirties, we care so much about what the Joneses think, even if we think we don't. These two decades are the time when we're most tempted to try to live for others. Around forty, it occurs to us that the Joneses are either going to like us or they're not, that the Joneses have holes in their socks too, thank you, and that we have less control over what other people think than we ever imagined.

And other people shouldn't have so much control over what we think either. There's too much "you should . . . you should not" told to women these days. Whether a woman takes hormones, wants to have a face-lift, wants to admit her age, or wants to talk about menopause is nobody's business but her own. There's privacy in a woman's heart that should never be violated, and certainly not in the name of feminism. We are doing the best we can. Whatever we come up with on our journey to expanded consciousness, let us have and let us be. What's going on inside us matters; everything else is cosmetic and should be treated as such. Once we remember we're cosmic queens, these issues won't arise. That's the only solution to all our shallow traumas.

We can stop trying so hard to win love and power

and influence in the world, because on some days we'll have those things and on others we won't. But if we look to them for sustenance, we will find despair. And growing more desperate, we will grow old. Age appalls us because maturity appalls us, responsibility appalls us. Our thirties are the time to get serious about being an adult, taking responsibility for our communities and our families. Our forties become the time for getting good at those things, for achieving some mastery. In our fifties, we should be able to shine. People in their fifties are like full-bodied wine. In our sixties and seventies, we could, in addition to shining, start teaching others, those coming up after us, how to do what we have done.

WITHOUT A SPIRITUAL LIFE, what are we left with? What is there to strive for? Where do we look for clues? In magazines?

Here are some basics for spiritual renewal. First of all, meditate. Do transcendental meditation (my favorite), Christian meditation, Jewish meditation, Buddhist meditation, open-eye meditation, full-moon meditation, Quaker meditation—it doesn't matter. Just do it. Also, pray. Engage in some sort of daily spiritual practice—nonreligious, religious, whatever. Above all else, try to forgive. And lastly, treat your body well. Practice yoga or some equivalent form of concentrated physical exercise.

Do not look to your husband, your lover, your children, your job, your money, or your therapist to make you happy. It's not their function, nor within their capacity to do so. Look to yourself, to the Goddess within you, and take responsibility for your own state of mind.

Women can be masters at negative programming. We constantly tell ourselves what is not right: our figure, our hair, our relationship, our job, the weather, someone else's behavior. Sometimes, we do this because we have legitimate complaints; at other times, we criticize simply because it is the turn of our minds to do so. Every time we do, regardless of why, we attack ourselves. We are programming our subconscious—the part of the mind that hears what we tell it and then creates more of the same—to manufacture the life we're describing. And then—magicians that we are—lo and behold, we have a new, even more negative life the following day.

Someone once gave me a coffee mug on which is printed ENTERTAIN NO NEGATIVITY. If only I could be so strong. As 1992 was drawing to a close and I gathered with friends at the approach of midnight, I scribbled on a piece of paper, "In 1993, I will repeat no negative stories." We are not a little powerful; we are enormously powerful. Every time we say a negative word, we lay the mental plans for negative things. There is no escaping this law of the mind. As we think, so shall it be.

Here's another helpful hint. Choose an affirmation that fits you, your hopes and your desires. Try to stay away from specifics, and concentrate instead on the woman you want to be. You could say, "I am a glorious child of God. I am joyful, serene, positive, and loving." Write it on several pieces of paper. Pin them up in your house or tape them to the dashboard of your car. The mind is more powerful than are any external conditions. If you repeat your affirmation ten times a day, particularly in combination with meditation, your life will change.

Spiritual techniques cannot not work. The question is not whether they work but whether or not we actually *do* them. If we remind ourselves often of the woman we want to be, then the woman who has been masquerading as us all these years will breathe her last breath and give us back our life.

On the days when I do these things—and having turned forty myself, I have finally learned how important it is to do them all—I feel good. On the days when I don't do them, I don't feel as well. And I must admit that there are often days during the month when nothing makes me happy, and that's it. PMS is PMS. Chemical depression is an even harder nut to crack. There are times and conditions when despite our exercises, we continue to cry and we continue to feel pain. I'm talking here about the broad strokes, the vast majority of our days. Try those things—meditation, prayer, yoga, affirmations—and the fabric of your life will become more beautiful and peaceful.

At times, we can find sustenance in a spiritual retreat, a woman's retreat, a vacation, a time off. It's important to have the chance to get away from it all.

But we must remember that the serenity and peace a retreat provides should not be limited to our time away from home; we must commit ourselves to incorporating the conditions that foster peace and serenity into our daily lives. So much inside us can flourish when we turn off the worldly noise. The search for inner peace is a life-style decision. Even when we have children, they can learn that at certain hours Mommy needs quiet time.

As much as we crave the rest a vacation offers, we often resist it. Many of us have set up our lives so that we are constantly busy, living on a kind of adrenaline that poses as energy. This is an insidious trick of the negative mind: building a wall of frantic activity that mitigates the experience of a meaningful inner life. We lose a tremendous amount of personal power and healthy energy by allowing ourselves to be lured away from daily spiritual practice. The spiritual life is our inner life, and a woman is lost without her connection to the God and Goddess within her.

As for physical appearance—as we age, gorgeous young hunks may or may not be interested in us anymore. For that matter, men our own age and older might not be interested anymore. My response to that is "So what?" We could have met up with these same guys when we were young, and they would still have been turned off to us anyway once we got older.

Have faith in men. There's a new breed forming, just as we're a new breed of women. They are quite young, some of them, and they are older also. They are learning, they are growing, and they are everywhere. Hold on. Just take care of yourself. Strive to live a more loving, more beautiful life. They won't not find you. Your appeal is huge and invisible and real.

What now? Agreements. Agreements that we will not hurt one another, that we will support one another. We will protect the children and heal the earth. We will make love an art, and we will love like artists.

A woman is meant to hold the heart of the world within her hands. She must cater to it and minister to it and kiss it when it cries. We are meant to keep the home fires burning, the fires in our hearts. We are meant to prepare the food, the spiritual food of love and compassion. We are meant to care for the children, not just our own, but every child. When we do not recognize our cosmic function, our own hearts break, and so does the heart of the world.

Just as children grow by playing games in which they imagine themselves to be grown-ups, so are we meant to grow by imagining ourselves to be bigger than we are right now. You need not apologize for being brilliant, talented, gorgeous, rich, or smart. Your success doesn't take away from anyone else's. It actually increases the possibility that others can have it too. Your money increases your capacity to give money to others, your joy increases your capacity to give joy to others, and your love increases your capacity to give love to others. Your playing small serves no one. It is a sick game. It is old thinking, and it is dire for the planet. Stop it immediately. Come home to the castle.

FOUR

Embracing the Goddess

A true conception of the relation between the sexes will not admit of conqueror and conquered; it knows but of one great thing; to give of one's self boundlessly, in order to find one's self richer, deeper, better.

—Emma Goldman

The story of many modern relationships is a variation on a common theme: the conspiracy between men and women to murder the Queen. Whenever a woman sells herself cheap or a man is unkind to a woman or a woman gives her body where she is not adored or a man rejects his true love—we are trying to murder the Queen. But the Queen is eternal; she cannot die. She can be tortured, but she cannot die.

A friend recently spoke to me of a very powerful man on the East Coast who has gained a reputation for toying cruelly with the hearts of so-called powerful women. The question, of course, is how does a powerful woman allow herself to be toyed with? What place of wounded self-esteem makes her vulnerable to his emotionally sadistic machinations? Perhaps, suggested my friend, I would address this question in my book.

"My book will not be about that," I told her. "That man is a dinosaur. His breed will die out." Thousands of us have been in therapy, taken seminars, read extensively, and explored all other means to personal growth in the last several years in order to learn how to avoid those guys. We've prayed. We've been on our knees. Where were those women? Go into therapy. Go to a good bookstore. The buzz words now are *recovery, wellness, bringing back joy.*

There's a great story about recovering from attraction to dangerous men. It goes like this: When you're really ill, you don't even know a snake when you see one. Once recovery begins, you see a snake and you know it's a snake, but you still play with it. Once you've landed in true recovery zone, you see a snake, you know it's a snake, and you cross to the other side of the road.

Until then, everyone you know can tell you the game is toxic with that person, but you won't listen because you think you're different or that he'll be different with you, or that maybe you're the first one to have really seen his sensitive side. There's no forcing the process by which we simply stop being attracted to pain. It's a long road for some of us. It's work. It takes deeper thinking and more courage than many of us are used to. But it's going on everywhere. It's the *real* liberation, and there aren't a lot of excuses in today's world for not joining in the work that will ultimately free us all.

There's not much mystery here. Sickness is not that interesting. When you were a little girl, Daddy told you in various ways that you weren't really all that great, so that any man who gives you the same message years later feels to you like the one you belong with. He's familiar in that he's remote and slightly disapproving. And the more we look, the more we realize that it wasn't just Daddy who went weird on us around the time we reached puberty. The whole world did. Our burgeoning sexuality didn't just freak out Daddy, who was attracted and repelled at the same time. It freaked out Mommy too, who was jealous, and our teachers, who had similar projections. It freaked out the entire society in which we grew up, because sex is still thought of as evil here. As we grew more and more into our womanhood, we were perceived as being more and more dangerous. None of this was conscious on anyone's part. Very little *is* conscious in this society or anywhere. The whole human race is still basically in a fog, but that's why we're here, and it's definitely why we're looking into this painful stuff that's been ruling us subconsciously for ages.

WOMEN ARE VERY CONFUSED about power, and actually, so are men. Feminine power isn't something we go out and acquire; it's already within us. It's something we become willing to experience. Something to admit we have.

Until we do, our positive power lies unexpressed. It's there, but it's not working. We're wired for something we don't know how to access. Having been taught that the power of strong women is in various ways suspect, many of us find it hard to fully embrace our power. We're afraid. But the Goddess is ready to correct our thinking. Her key, the access point, the miracle, is love. We are here only to love, and love casts out fear. When we understand that love is the reason for our power—that it *is* our power—we lose our fear of owning its strength. We become willing to experience the power within us, that it might be used as a channel through which love is expressed to all humankind.

And so, powerful women fall prey to the East Coast lady-killer not because he's consciously seeking to murder the Queen but because they are. Not having embraced her themselves, they find no one else to embrace her either. They are stuck in princess mode, crying and tearing their hair out, shouting "You can't treat me this way" when, quite obviously, he sure can. Until we own our own power, we will constantly seek it in others, particularly in men, and power sought that way never saves us; it destroys us.

Many women complain that they keep attracting the "wrong relationship." What they mean by that, of course, is that they are attracted *to* the wrong relationship. They are stuck in a place that is dangerous but seductive. They want desperately to get out of the pattern but often not quite desperately enough. They lack the self-esteem to save their own lives.

We give up what we want to give up and keep what in some way we still want to keep. There are payoffs for holding on to small, weak patterns. We have an excuse not to shine. We don't have to take responsibility for the world when we're spending all our time in emotional pain. We're too busy. The truth that sets us free is an embrace of the divine within us. It means remembering we are the daughters of God, and daughters of God don't brake for jerks.

When a woman falls in love with the magnificent possibilities within herself, the forces that would limit those possibilities hold less and less sway over her. A relationship that keeps us tied to the push and pull of co-dependent neuroses is a block to our shining. When we are very clear that we *want* to shine—and if we want to know the Goddess, we want to shine—then we attract into our lives the kinds of relationships that help us do that. Until a woman has given herself permission to be fabulous, she will not find herself with partners who promote her ability to be so. As long as she tears herself down, she will attract others who tear her down; she will find people who agree that she is undeserving and lacking as long as that is how she thinks of herself.

So we're left with a commitment to being a certain kind of woman before worrying about finding a certain kind of man. Once we make such a commitment, good guys will appear. Until we do, let's just say they're waiting in the lobby.

Embrace the Goddess and her divine perception of you. Ask her to reveal to you the you she has in mind. Ask her to send you the relationships and circumstances that will foster that strength within you, that the world might be blessed by the presence of a woman in all her glory. Ask and you'll receive. Don't ask, and you'll continue to receive the relationships that destroy you. Until we embrace the light, we remain vulnerable to darkness. The choice is easy once we see it for what it is. In relationships, as in everything else, we ask for heaven, or we ask for hell.

SEVERAL YEARS AGO, my boyfriend left me for a bimbo. Actually, he didn't leave me, and according to quite a few people she's not a bimbo. But my emotional experience, as arrogant and unenlightened as it was, was that I had been rejected for someone half my size.

It's not uncommon for an intelligent man to gravitate toward a woman who can't quite put a sentence together. But why does it happen? I wanted to find out because the pain I felt was searing. I knew in my heart that I had blown something big-time, and I wanted to correct myself. I would have done anything and gone anywhere to learn what I needed to before I went out again. Some of the clearest thinking we do about relationships occurs while we're not in one. We're humbler, more in touch with our pain, more teachable.

Our intelligence is always sharper when informed by our own feelings.

At another point in my life, I lived a scene like the one at the end of the movie *Gone With the Wind*, where Scarlett asks Rhett what's to become of her if he leaves her. In my case, the man did give a damn, but he still had to leave. I then had to prove to myself, and to whomever else I thought might care, that I could make it without him. Imagine another scene, the one in which Scarlett says, "I will never go hungry again." My pledge, uttered with the same strength and anguish, was "I will never need a man again."

That was a flawed decision.

I couldn't have him, so I became him. I wanted him within me so badly I invoked his energy from within myself. I conquered outer worlds, just as he had. I expressed masculine strength and power, just as he had. But it didn't bring me closer to him or to others like him because I had become one of the guys, and that's not what most men are looking for. He had never loved me for being a great guy.

I don't know when my mourning set in, but I know it climaxed when I lost out to the woman I thought was a bimbo. What I realized was that she was in some ways the old me—not the me I wanted to become but the me I had been and then left behind. She wasn't stupid; I just wanted to think she was. And that's why I had to hate her. I couldn't bear to take on all the hatred I felt toward myself for becoming so masculine and tough.

I started to understand what had gone wrong, including the realization that I was far from alone in my predicament. And it wasn't enough just to understand. I had to retrain myself, which I'm still doing. I don't want to lose the masculine power I've developed, the worldly effectiveness, the power to act on things I care about. It's part of me and an important aspect of who we all are. It was certainly a necessary social development for women to actualize their masculine power in the world.

But I needed to put things in their proper perspective. In intimate relationships with men, I want to major in feminine and minor in masculine. At a lecture podium, I'm the masculine, active energy to the audience's feminine receptiveness. After work, if I'm with a man I am close to, I want to experience myself as a woman. And I no longer kid myself that it would work for him, or for me, to play it any differently. That doesn't mean we don't trade roles at times. It means the dominant groove is that he's masculine and I'm feminine.

The masculine is active, the feminine passive; the masculine is dynamic, the feminine magnetic. The masculine *does* while the feminine *is*. Part of our Amazon neurosis is the way we have all learned to play the man: to go to him before he comes to us, to call first, to make the first move. Only now do we realize what a mistake that is, and we're having to tie our hands behind our backs, bite our tongues, sit on our credit cards.

Most of us want a masculine man, but there's no way to have one unless we become feminine women. At first, we're outraged to realize this because we thought we were being such good girls by developing our masculine side to begin with. That's what we thought real worth, real power was. We came to see women—usually beginning with Mommy—as weak and ineffective, so we wanted to grow up and be just like Daddy. And God help us, we did.

During the sixties, male and female development was changing as our parents took what they thought was a more liberated approach to raising their sons and daughters. Daddy slapped his little girl on the back when she achieved something in the world, telling her how proud he was—and meaning it. He didn't know what to do with the girl stuff anyway, since the feelings it brought up inside him were so threatening. We were moving into a new, modern era. The sexes would be equal. Girls were liberated—to be just like boys!

When I was growing up, my father was a well-known immigration lawyer and my mother a house-wife. My father was given constant kudos for his admirable contributions to the lives of poor and strug-gling immigrants. My mother, as far as I was con-cerned, did not participate meaningfully in the world at all. At the time, I could not see that driving kids to ballet class, scheduling Girl Scout meetings, or sewing doll clothes was important work. Today, I see things very differently. I see I was one of thousands of young girls who unconsciously decided that our mothers' lives were meaningless, while our fathers' lives were glamorous and important. The way to succeed, it seemed to us, was to grow up and be just like Daddy.

So, I created a career for myself not unlike my father's. When I started lecturing on *A Course in Miracles* in the early eighties, I found myself surrounded by people burdened with serious problems. I met many people with HIV-positive infections and other life-challenging illnesses. I was thrown into a world in which other people were hurting more than I was, and the moral as well as professional imperative was that I be the strong one and hold other people up. Unconsciously, I had created a career just like Daddy's. I had become what in Jungian terms is called a father's daughter.

I learned early on to apply discipline to my professional endeavors. Week after week, month after month, and year after year, I showed up at prayer groups, lectures, support groups, hospital rooms, marriages, funerals. I founded organizations, had a child, and wrote a book. I knew I had to be strong, and I thought strength didn't cry. I had seen my father's lack of emotion as strength and my mother's show of emotion as weakness. I wanted to be strong like my father. I couldn't break down at the funeral if I was the one conducting the service. If a mother was grieving for her son, I couldn't cave in. I wanted to be a shoulder for her to lean on. I didn't want to do anything that would threaten my ability to be strong in my role of mother hen. What I didn't understand was that I had become not a mother hen but a father hen.

Although I was driven by tender emotions, I thought that expressing them fully might limit my power. I built a wall that would hold my emotions at bay, thinking I needed to do that in order to best serve others. It took a lot of willpower to build that wall, but I can see now that it did not take strength. The denial of emotion through suppression or withdrawal is a weak move, not a courageous one.

So this is the Amazon neurosis: the woman who achieves at the expense of her tender places. From the time she was a little girl, she was slowly but surely led to believe that her emotions were less important than her achievements, perhaps even antithetical to them. And the love she received in response to her achievements, if it was love at all, is not the love that warms the night.

A woman who cannot honor her own feelings will not find them honored by anyone else. Other people will find her hard to penetrate. I have experienced this in diverse and painful ways. When I began to recognize what a high personal price I paid for dissociating myself from my own feelings, I did what I had to do to let them up and out. Lots of therapy, lots of work, lots of pain. And then, sure enough, just as I had feared, I began to lose my grip. I conducted a funeral service for someone I had hardly known, and I couldn't stop crying as I gave my talk. But this was just a temporary phase. I moved on through the weepy period and came out at the other end stronger and more tender, less guarded and more available.

USUALLY WHEN we think of power, we think of external power, and we think of powerful people as those who have made it in the world. A powerful woman isn't necessarily someone who has money, but we think of her as someone with a boldness or a spark that makes her manifest in a dramatic way. When we think of a powerful man, we think of his ability to manifest abundance—usually money—in the world.

Most people say that a powerful woman does best with a powerful man, that she needs someone who understands the bigness of her situation, a man who can meet her on the same or a greater level of power in the world. This is true if power is defined as material abundance. A woman often faces cultural prejudice when she makes more money than a man, as does he. A woman who defines power by worldly standards can rarely feel totally relaxed in the arms of a man who doesn't have it.

If power is seen as an internal matter, then the situation changes drastically. Internal power has less to do with money and worldly position and more to do with emotional expansiveness, spirituality, and conscious living. As we begin to recognize that internal strength is all that really matters, we come to see that we have often avoided men who were not powerful in the world not because they were not powerful enough, but because inwardly they were too powerful, reminding us of the work we still had to do on ourselves.

I used to think that I needed a "powerful man," someone who could protect me from the harshness and evils of the world. What I have come to realize is that the evils of the world that confront me are a reflection of my own internal state, and no one can protect me from my own mind. The powerful man I was looking for would be, foremost, someone who supported me in keeping on track spiritually and in so maintaining clarity within myself that life would pose fewer problems. When it did get rough, he would help me forgive.

I no longer want someone who would say to me, "Don't worry, honey. If they're mean to you, I'll beat them up or buy them out." Instead, I want someone who prays and meditates with me regularly so that fewer monsters from the outer world disturb me, and who, when they do, helps me look within my own consciousness for answers instead of looking to false power to combat false power.

There's a big difference between a weak man and a gentle man. Weak men make us nervous. Gentle men make us calm.

MANY OF US have desired, or do desire, marriage. How much of our desire is natural, and how much of it is cultural? What is natural is our desire for the beloved. What is cultural is our tendency to forget that a piece of paper cannot tie hearts together. The issue is not whether we marry, but whether we allow any choice of life-style to impinge on our ability to fly.

What is important, if we do choose to marry, is that we not give up our wilder spirits. I once heard someone say that married women can't write. I don't think this is true, but I understand what it means. Marriage is not a mere convention but it is often lived as one and, as such, will sink instead of uplift a woman's spirit. The creative spirit thrives on freedom and daring. Many of history's most creative women have not been married. As for the priestesses of olden times, don't even think about it. Priestesses were spiritual mermaids, and a lot of men were drowning.

Patriarchal culture senses danger in the unmarried woman. If a man is unmarried, he is called a bachelor. If a woman is unmarried, she is called a spinster or an old maid. What is it about an unmarried woman that poses such a threat to the patriarchal order? Mainly, it is that women are no one's property when we're unmarried. We're under no one's control, and neither are our children. There is no telling what we might do or say.

Much of the prejudice against women is stored at an unconscious level. Many of those who hold the most punishing attitudes toward passionate women—and free women are passionate women—consider themselves social liberals, even feminists. Women's rights seem to them to be of obvious importance, but what is not obvious to them is how much they themselves conspire to keep the lid on female power.

Female power transcends what are known politically as women's issues. Female power has to do with
women taking an active part in the conversation—
whether in the public arena or at the dinner table—
and having the same emotional space in which to do
so as men. It means women not having to fear punishment of any kind. It means women not having to
worry that we'll be considered unfeminine if we speak
up. It means women really coming out to play and
getting support for our playing—from men as well as
from women. Until this is accomplished, political, economic, and reproductive freedoms will not be
enough. We will not be free until we can speak our
minds and our hearts without having to worry that
men will crucify us, women will crucify us, the press
will crucify us, or our children will be ashamed.

The true politics of women's liberation is human
politics. It is under the surface, the energy in a room—
not in the bedroom, because there we won freedom as
soon as it was discovered how much more fun life is
when we are in the game. But outside the bedroom,
we are still not equal partners, and until we are, the
world will not be healed. Women are still in emotional
bondage as long as we need to worry that we might
have to make a choice between being heard and being
loved.

After the Anita Hill–Clarence Thomas showdown
on Capitol Hill, a friend told me an interesting story.
She had watched the televised hearings with several
married couples. Except for herself and two others,

the women in attendance remained silent. Their husbands, on the other hand, held forth on how shameful it all was, expressing their perfect liberal views with seemingly no awareness of what was going on in that very room. Their wives behaved like good little girls: they sat by quietly, allowing their husbands to sound brilliant and insightful.

Would things have been different had the couples not been married? I don't know. What is operative in this case is not marriage but the connection between women and men itself. What needs to be addressed is who we are in partnership. Whether we are married matters less and less today as the definition of marriage changes along with everything else around us. What I think is relevant in this story is not that the couples were married but that they were in public. Behind closed doors, perhaps each of these husbands shows great respect for his wife.

What is still lacking in American society is permission for women to speak up in public—loudly and clearly—without being considered ball breakers. Let's look at that name one more time: *ball breaker*. Try to come up with an expression that conjures more of an association with male pain. It's almost impossible. Now try to come up with an expression more often associated with a woman who speaks her mind. Most women faced with the choice of hurting men or shutting up go back to sleep and sleep forever.

Women and men are now obviously relearning our roles vis-à-vis one another, both in marriage and out of it. Several years ago, I was leading a weekend seminar when the subject of marriage came up. I asked how many people in the group were married and then asked them to express their thoughts about it. As the group of thirty or so talked late into the night, I heard things that surprised me. I realized that weekend, and became more and more aware during subsequent sessions of counseling married as well as unmarried couples, that marriage is whatever people make of it. And it is detrimental to all of us to hold narrow, formulaic pictures of what that should be.

I have heard married couples who describe their conjugal relationships as very, very happy, in monogamous as well as in open marriages. I have heard married couples who describe their conjugal relationships as boring and unhappy, in monogamous as well as in open marriages. Sex is a sacrament, not a prison. While monogamy can be a beautiful, even sacred bond, it might not be the agreement that best suits everyone. Our thinking that monogamy is inherently a nobler arrangement than any other has created a nation of hypocrites—which is what we've become.

Don't kid yourself. Historically, monogamy didn't begin as a way to ensure that two people could relax into the deepest intimacy. It began as a way for men to assert their ownership over a woman's body. In many cultures throughout history, and in some today, it is acceptable for men to have multiple partners but not for women to do the same. The value of monogamy and the persistence of the double standard are subjects that need to be discussed, by men as well as by women, in public and in private, in order to exorcise the sexual demons we still allow to control us. It is very difficult to be clear about what you want when your mind is overwhelmed by input about what you're supposed to want.

If you love a man—how wonderful if you do—and if you desire a monogamous union with him—how wonderful if you do—then marry him if your heart calls you to, and know that the union you have chosen can serve God and Goddess, and men and women. But never, ever—married or not—allow your partnership with a man to silence your voice or keep you from supporting another woman in using hers, or you are helping to perpetuate a most vicious muffling of a most beautiful sound. The world has no idea of the song we're not yet hearing: women singing out, in harmony with men and each other, at full blast, at full volume. It's music we need. Men long to hear it, and women long to join the choir.

Be very clear. The silence is a sick one.

IF MEN ONLY KNEW how much we have to say. But so often, we cannot speak. In the presence of resistance, we clam up. In the presence of approval, we blossom into goddesses.

There are times when we have to turn away from things that hold us back, and nothing holds us back like someone who invalidates who we are and what we're capable of. A young man is often brought up to think that he will one day find the right woman to support his vision and greatness. Many young girls are brought up to think that we will one day find a man whose vision and greatness are worthy of our support.

The ancient Greek word for courtesan is *hetaera*. The *hetaera* was a man's lover, his equal, and his muse. She carried his vision and made space for his brilliance. There is no such word for the correlative male position, although *husband* would be nice.

Who is to hold the space for a woman's greatness? In many heterosexual relationships, a man is threatened by a woman's greatness, finding a variety of ways to make her question her own beauty and strength. A secure man is not threatened by a woman's intellectual or emotional power but celebrates the opportunity for joyful partnership that it offers him. The conscious question is whether a relationship can handle two stars.

We must relinquish the paradigm of men as power with women as support and instead embrace the image of both men and women as powers, with each supporting the other. Any man who holds a woman back is not a man a woman can afford to be with. A woman has a mighty and sacred task to perform on earth. She will not be able to fulfill her function if she remains with a man who derides her glory.

Women are not powerless. We just pretend we are. We do this in large part because we are afraid of the punishment inflicted on us when we dare to be who we really are. It's a subtle form of discrimination, but it's clearly there. A few women are allowed into the club, it seems: women who have allowed themselves to be partially declawed, their sexual threat to the status quo diminished just enough, so that men and women alike can handle the juice. But an animal in the wild is not declawed, and an animal in the wild is a beautiful thing.

In the wild, we scream. We scream when we hurt, we scream when we give birth, we scream when we come, and that's just the way it is. Now what kind of man can handle our passion, and what kind of man can ascend to the throne next to a woman who owns her own crown? A princess attracts a prince, and a queen attracts a king. Women who whine attract men who whine. Women full of the lioness heart attract men who are full of the lion.

And this is where women are now, at a place where, perhaps for the first time ever, people are remembering en masse our cosmic function. Our love affairs are not here to serve an industrialist machinery or a government system. Our sex is not for procreation alone. Our love is here to spiritualize the earth. Both women and men are in quantum fast forward. We are growing new brains. We are using new eyes.

And when a woman remembers her glory, a man of goodwill can barely contain his joy. His real self arises in the presence of her own. I'm telling you, it works, this thing, this looking within to attract what is without. Make room for love, and it always comes. Make a nest for love, and it always settles. Make a home for the beloved, and he will find his way there.

FIVE

Sex and Soul

Be not ashamed, woman . . .
You are the gates of the body,
and you are the gates of the soul.

—Walt Whitman

When the enchanted woman has come into her power, then and only then has she the inner strength to turn her face toward someone else. Only then does she have the authority to meet another person's gaze and hold it.

A lover is a high-stakes proposition. He, or she,* is the best of all worlds, or the worst of all worlds. We have no capacity to deal with another person's power effectively until our own is pure and intact. Knowing

---

*I understand and respect that many women love other women. If you prefer the intimacy of other women, please forgive me for not writing "man or woman" each time I refer to a partner.

this, we begin to understand the relationship between our search for the self and our search for the beloved. For the Goddess inside us, there is no distinction between the two. The lover is not whom we hide behind; the lover is who appears before us as we emerge from the shadows of our own delusions. A goddess does not go and "get" a lover; she *is* a true lover, and happiness gathers unto her. Love is not something that comes into us from someone else; it is an extension of our own minds, reverberating back to us in what seems to be another person's smile.

A female who does not know these things is a primary candidate for wearing two emotionally wounded feminine faces: the woman we call doormat, and the woman we call bitch. Having lost her inner girl, she has for all practical purposes lost the experience of her own innocence. She can't remember why she is guilty, but she has been effectively convinced she is not OK. And full of conviction that she is far from perfect, she projects onto others—particularly those who have the audacity to draw close—that they are as imperfect as she and therefore just as deserving of punishment. This is when the bitch takes over. She will do to someone else the damage she is bent on doing to herself. She will punish them as she is so sure she deserves to be punished.

On the other hand, since she knows she's so bad, she thinks maybe she hasn't the right to do anything or say much or even live at all. And if all she is, is a hotbed of guilt, then all that is good will be seated outside her, and every so often it will seem to be seated in someone she meets. That other person, then, is given all the power, and the woman will lie there, quiet and docile, martyr to the evil that is rampant in her system. The classic doormat, the classic wimp. She will have no power to speak or assert herself. The other person will have taken it all. The other person has been given the right to hold the whip and do the whipping.

Yuk. How sick. Yet how familiar. Those demons are known to all of us, but we are not reading this now to get further acquainted. We are here now to meet the Goddess, to hear her thoughts and learn her techniques for meeting love in the light of day and fulfilling its promises late at night.

Let's linger no more over problems in love, except where they still need to be confronted. Let's instead map out the Goddess's way, of meeting a beloved and touching his soul and loving him with all her miraculous power.

WE USUALLY KNOW a lover is on the way well before he gets here. As often as we hear stories like "I met my partner when I least expected to meet anyone," on some level, we know that's nonsense. A woman in touch with herself can sense the coming of things, and the coming of love is like a deer running through a forest on the way to your door. We can feel a love approaching; and when we are in touch with the Goddess, we prepare ourselves in advance.

How do we do that? It is as if we were pregnant when we are about to meet a beloved: We are about to give birth to a new creative force. The highest preparation is a strengthening of our calm, a focusing of our clarity on who we are and what our values are. The core values—the ones that feed the lesser ones as a river feeds its tributaries—are those of love, forgiveness, and the desire to serve God. We serve him to the extent that we have thoughts of purity. Purity means that we do not manipulate or seduce or preprogram or project hidden agendas onto anyone or anything.

The Goddess is in her highest glory when we are in love. We are also the most tempted at that time to spit in her face and mock her virtue. Our highest work is to remember how important it is—for the world, for our spirits, for the relationship itself—that we learn to be a friend to our beloved and a spiritual companion to our beloved and provide a sense of home to those we love the most. Otherwise, we can look great, smell great, and use our bodies like the best of them; but without our virtue, we are whores and we will not know love.

Once we meet him, we'd better have our spiritual chops down, because the attraction—his smell, the chemistry between us—will tempt us to forget the truth if it's not a solid part of us already. If it is, then there is no higher high than that of the passionate love. I don't have sexually intimate relationships with women, but I assume they are the same joining. I do know that when a woman loves a man and opens to him and lets the spirit move her, the ride is a ride to the center of things. Our bodies don't just feel as though they melt, they *do* melt; and our spirits don't just feel as though they merge, they *do* merge.

We enter a divine room when the Goddess meets her consort and beckons him to enter. Her joyful hello is often "Hello, again!" for in that place we can remember that we've known each other before. How glad we are to be back whenever we find ourselves in love together. How lonely we have felt at times, and how ecstatic we are to spend some time at home.

How important it is to know that he is as tender as we are and just as lost and just as scared. Until we know this, we miss the point. We think he's such a monster, until we see he's such a boy. Like us, scarred from Daddy's whatever disaster; so too is he affected by Mommy forever. And all of us stumble and cry, and fall and seek in each other the relief from our pain. We are meant to be that relief and more than that. We are meant to be the healing of the wound; and if we will allow it, our love will heal us both.

Remember the eyes of one who loved you, and don't forget their mark on your soul. Carry it always, the badge of a woman who has opened her heart and allowed it to hurt, for herself and for him. She has gone crazy for love and been ridiculous for love and grown neurotic for love and wasted her time for love. But she has grown from the heartaches and endured until the sun shone, and finally she has seen the sky. Now she's a woman when before she was a girl; now she's a goddess when before she was a brat.

This is the journey of every woman who has loved a man. May we all find sustenance in knowing there's a remarkable prize waiting for us as we approach the truth. We are so lucky to be women, and those men are so lucky to know us. We are so full of miracles for all who come to us with pure and open hearts. We are so full of love for those who approach with tender souls. We are so full of beauty for those who believe it's there.

And men are such a gorgeous lot, the boys who made the climb from the arrogantly weak to the humbly strong. The initiate into the ways of love is like a letter from God telling us that he's here. The initiate, both man and woman, has seen a dark night and then seen another day. There is no substitute for the fires that purify us; whatever they were, they served a purpose. And now we will know how to love and be loved, and never again will we lose our way.

A WOMAN IN LOVE is drunk with something. There's a chemical syrup that permeates her cells, a place in her being where hormones meet God. It's hell or heaven or both. If we could harness its power, we could heal the world.

And that's the point. A woman in love can do anything. She can run a business, bear children, create art, make love, cook meals, lead a nation, and figure out how to look great. But if she is not in love, she lacks energy; and if she is in love but spurned, she can lack the will to live. Women need to be in love: with themselves, with a man, with a child, with a project, with a job, with their country, with the planet, and—most important—with life itself. Women in love are closer to enlightenment. For angels and lovers, everything sparkles.

Our love is not co-dependency. Co-dependency is what happens when we don't know how to apply our love, where to put it, what to do with it. Most men have no idea of the lengths to which a woman will go for love or the depths of our despair when we feel it cut off. This is not to say that men don't fly high or crash tragically. Of course they do. But their love doesn't fuel the world the way ours does. Their love is the car; ours is the gas.

The only beloved who can always be counted on is God. The ultimate partner is a divine one, an experience of ourselves that is totally supportive and forgiving. Until we know this, we keep seeking sustenance from men that they cannot give us. Most men and women today are wounded. The search for someone who isn't in pain is unreasonable until we ourselves are healed of our own dysfunctions. Until then, we will be led to people as wounded as we are in order that we might heal and be healed together. What this means is that no partner can save us, deliver us, or give meaning to our lives. The source of our salvation, deliverance, and meaning is within us. It is the love we give as much as it is the love we get. The passion we most need to feed is our relationship to God. This is ultimately our relationship to ourselves.

It's not as easy as a good date, as much fun as sex, or as dramatic as romantic tension. It is work. Personal growth, recovery, religious practice, spiritual renewal—whatever words we care to use—these are the keys to our return to sanity and peace. When we have reclaimed our wholeness, we are ready to face the worldly beloved. Until then, we will look to a romantic partner to give us peace rather than remember that our role in the relationship is to *bring* peace, by receiving it from God and allowing him to spread his peace through us to all humankind.

How often I have betrayed myself, forgetting—or, more accurately, resisting—the twenty minutes of meditation, the hour of reading, the spiritual meeting or recovery group that would prepare me for the roller coaster ride that always lies potential in an intimate relationship. Part of our problem is that we expect love affairs to always feel good. They don't. Actually, relationships don't feel good anyway. *We* feel good. Unless we are centered within ourselves, we cannot blame a relationship for throwing us off. No man can convince a woman she's wonderful, but if she already believes she is, his agreement can resonate and bring her joy.

This is our function in each others' lives: to hold the space for each other's beauty, that our beloved can leave us and we still feel in his absence how beautiful we are.

• • •

MOST WOMEN TODAY are borderline hysterical. We are loudly hysterical or quietly hysterical. Our despair is acted out externally, or it cuts through our bodies in the form of physical illness. We are desperate to find serenity and peace.

When we were taught as children, and most of us were, that our value lies in what we do as opposed to who we are, we automatically switched to a masculine psychological mode—doing, doing, doing—in order to feel worthy. There seems to be no value placed on the experience of inner peace, and without it we find no room in which to rest. This leaves men as well as women feeling spiritually homeless.

I have a friend, Gwen, a woman about my age who has contracted a rare and particularly vicious form of cancer. At one of my support groups, when the subject of death came up, she said that she had been obsessed with thoughts of dying since she was a little girl. Her life as a child had been hideous, and her only idea of a possible escape was through physical death.

Her psychoimmunologist had told her before we met—and I agree—that her body has merely caught up with her mind. But I know this girl, and it behooves all women to be clear about the reason she felt so alien in this world that she wanted to die. Gwen is the essence of a certain kind of femininity, all gossamer and fairylike. She is the kind of woman we read about when we escape into books of tales about Merlin and enchanted castles. It's not that women like that don't exist anymore. But they are the girls who have the hardest time today, who so often become deeply depressed while young, get cancer while young, and die while young.

These girls don't make it. They wither and die. Fish can't make it without water, astronauts can't make it without space suits, and enchanted women can't make it without love and a sense of the miraculous. Period. We live in an environment hostile to sensitive souls. Sometimes, the reason the good die young is that they don't want to hang out here any longer than is absolutely necessary.

So I said to Gwen, "You didn't really want to die when you were a child. What you wanted to do was to *live*. You just didn't know that the world you were living in was a living death."

We know so little in this society about the search for enlightenment, and what's worse is that in our pugnacious arrogance we often look down on those who do know something about it. We have squeezed the mystical experience out of our cultural data bank. And millions and millions of starved souls are reaching for it anyway, lining up in fervent pilgrimage. Women are at the forefront of the spiritual hunger march. Why? Because it is our only hope.

Back to Gwen and her cancer. At every meeting, as she lay her painfully skinny body against pillows on the floor because a chair was too hard for her to sit on, there was next to her, every time, a handsome man. He was her boyfriend, Daniel, obviously healthy and devoted to her healing. What a good sight: a man concerned for a woman's pain, there for her through the thick of it, sharing this time of crisis as if it were his own. When human beings stand by one another, testify to their faith, and witness each other's pain, miracles happen. If we are loved enough, we are emotionally healed and spiritually made whole.

There is a little bit of Gwen in all of us, struggling to deal with the pain of our predicaments yet holding on to the love we've found, knowing it's the only thing that can save us. Gwen and Daniel struggle, as do every woman and every man, with the questions that illuminate the fundamental issues of life: Why are we here? How do we heal? Are we, in fact, our brother's keeper? We might not be our brother's keeper, but we are definitely his mother, his sister, his daughter. For his sake and for ours, we must begin to say no to the diseases that threaten to kill us. Some of them stalk our bodies, and some of them stalk our souls.

I ONCE TOLD A LOVER that I would write a book of poems for him and called it *Severely Laid*. Now I would write another book and call it *Sincerely Touched*. It probably would not be interesting to anyone but me, since the rocky road to peace is more sensational than peace itself, and the yearning for love is more dramatic when it hurts.

Until we get to the point where we've had enough of things that hurt and long more than anything for a peaceful love, we are bound to take painful roads. We are destined to play out our frivolous disasters until we declare ourselves finished and done with them. How much pain do we have to suffer before we are sure we want no more? As much, it seems, as we have to until we don't. We just get tired, or we get reborn, when we have suffered so much that we have started to die.

The scars on our hearts do not last forever. They are the temporary signs of a tender soul who has touched the earth and been burned by such a low descent. Once the earth has been redeemed and our relationships are returned to God, the scars within us will be miraculously healed. But until we know the source of true healing, we will continue to go down, and we will continue to hurt. This is endurable until we are no longer young, but even the young grow old if our hearts are blasted hard enough and often.

What holy thought can spur us on when we feel too sick to try again? The thoughts of God are not so distant. The truth is there when the mind is ready to receive it. As soon as prayers are lifted up, the heart begins to rise and mend. There are many books and many teachers. So many new friends arrive when we stop making love to enemies.

As soon as we have chosen to do so, we can see each other not as we were but as we would be. We can choose to see the goodness in each other, to be loyal friends, to forgive and support. The sight of our innocence is the experience of light. We know the darkness: how to condemn, how to judge. The pain we felt there was a symptom of our sickness, a sign that we had turned away from love.

Love is not a cool arrangement or a night in bed. Love is angels hovering, circling, calling us to seek the sky together. And when we do, we change our patterns. We become new women; we become new men. And then we can go back to bed and laugh and howl as we used to do, but with much more joy and such relief.

Our goal in love is to love like queens, showing up not as girls but as women, with faith and charity and purity of heart. Love is very serious business. It takes a powerful heart to invoke it clearly and prepare for its coming.

We must recognize the perniciousness of our predominant cultural imagery. Everywhere we look we are presented with the idea that men toy with women, women toy with men—that's just the way things are; it's the way of love. But that is not the way of love; it's the way of lovelessness. How often we seek love but leave love out. We don't think about being kind and caring, we think about how we can hook a man. We don't think about his fears and his problems, we think of our own and how we can get him to solve them. We don't think about him period—but about his money, his body, his job, or his connections.

Perhaps these mistakes don't apply to you. But if they apply at all to any thoughts that ever enter your mind, then know the universe is taping your every thought and playing them back to some council in the sky. Consider it all recorded in some book they keep and tally up. And we suffer according to the level of our bullshit. Exploitative thoughts are not pure, and our function on earth is to reach for some pure state. Until we do, the pain will endure.

Sorry, girls, I never said this would be easy.

Dear God, we have wandered in the desert for so long, cut off from each other and from ourselves. Never again need we go back to worn-out patterns of cruelty and betrayal. From this day forward, let us love anew and become like new and forever laugh. Let the devil, whatever we call his power, be cast into hell and never get out again, never stalk our streets again and never poison our wells again. We have found the key that opens the gate, and we enter the garden of our father's house. We are comforted, and we are released at last. We smile at our brothers, embrace our sisters. They have made it too. No one remains outside the gate—only the devil is there, and he can reach us no more.

SOME MEN KNOW how to love a woman, and some men don't. Some men know that a light touch of the tongue, running from a woman's toes to her ears, lingering in the softest way possible in various places in between, given often enough and sincerely enough, would add immeasurably to world peace. Add to that pertinent conversation about political events, history, philosophy, art, and—most particularly—your feelings and hers, and you've got the stuff that makes a woman happy. It sounds relatively easy, this prescription for pleasing a woman, because it is. Do not tear her down. Do not ignore her. Do tell her she is beautiful and wonderful and precious. Do kiss her often and caress her shoulders.

Give us a little, and we fly. Give us the things I just told you about, give them consistently and do not get caught up with drugs, alcohol, or any similar obsessions, and you will not believe the way we soften. Our hearts melt when we're loved; and when we're loved the way I'm telling you, we're the best, the most wonderful, the most lovable creatures.

When love goes wrong, terrible chemical reactions occur in our cells. They cause illness and hysteria and deep, deep sadness. We feel as if a dark ink has spilled through our emotional veins when we are toyed with or our hearts are crushed or our sexuality is mocked. Our womanhood is major business. When it is treated like a minor issue, we burn.

IN BED, we want to surrender. We want to feel he's bigger, stronger, on top, in charge, and that he could be tough if he had to be. Outside of bed, we want the opposite. How dare he be bigger, stronger, on top, in charge, or even a hint of tough.

There is obvious confusion here. Surrender isn't a losing position in bed, and it's actually not a losing position outside of bed, either. But we can see this only when we're clear that surrender doesn't mean giving up or giving in. Surrender is not loss. To surrender is not to capitulate. To surrender basically just means to relax and let someone else have his or her own strength.

A lover used to say to me, "Surrender, Dorothy," whenever I would get too pumped up and full of myself. When we surrender, we don't surrender to a man. We surrender to a part of ourselves that is softer, less controlling, more interested in peace than in argument. It's not a game we play; it's a dance we do.

And the truth is we all want to so badly. For a lot of us, it feels like a dirty secret at first to admit this. We're afraid not to toe the party line. God forbid we should say, "I want to surrender." We might be labeled retro-ites, backlashers, the ones who would send us back into the kitchen instead of forward to the White House.

But it is not regressive to surrender to our feminine selves. It's the most progressive line of development because it honors, instead of represses, our emotions. We're definitely headed for the White House, please God, and to Congress, the state house, the mayor's office, the boardroom, and every other seat of worldly power. But when we get there, we must arrive as women, not men in drag. Being a woman means much more than just having a vagina.

The feminine force is intuitive, nurturing, the connecting glue. The feminine is a place inside us where we're receptive rather than active. In this country and on this planet, humans have everything we need in order to heal the world and live happy lives. We have information, technology, skills, money, intelligence, and scientific ability. What we are lacking is a meaningful relationship among these things. We have knowledge but little understanding. We lack context. We lack the conscious intention to use our resources for the purposes of love and healing. And without this, we cannot go anywhere. We are like a 747 without fuel.

Love is our fuel. It gives grace to progress and blessing to our will for power. We fail in our deepest responsibility to God and to ourselves each time we fail to declare love and act on love and witness to love. As women, we must keep this message alive. We must understand its importance and relay it to others, whispering it in the dark and shouting it in the light of day. Yes, it is time for women to enter the worldly mainstream. But not in such a way that we contribute to the power that produces without meaning or strives forward without love of humanity in mind. Let the word go out and grow stronger within: The love in our hearts is the power that matters.

Let technology serve our love for one another and not our mutual destruction. Let intelligence lead us to peace and not to war. Let our money be used to heal and not to further wound. We must understand these words. They must become part of who we are. This is the song of the Goddess as she makes her way across the earth. Sing with her, or lose your voice.

• • •

THE PURPOSE OF LOVE is to find a partner we can grow with, through the barriers that keep love at bay, to the center of the universe that exists inside all of us. Getting past the barriers, those walls that surround our hearts, means hanging around long enough to get a look at what they are. We must work to find God, not to find men. Women must stop trying to be good enough, except for God. People judge us; God doesn't. When we listen to God, it's very clear to us that we're more than good enough already. We learn from God that we're absolutely glorious—in his image, for his sake.

Ultimately, we learn to stop trying so hard. We no longer try to get a guy when we remember we're only here to bless him. There is a difference between *getting* a partner and *attracting* a partner. *Getting* implies that our hooks work; *attracting* means that our light is bright and appears like a beacon to one who is meant to see it. When we try to get a partner, we increase our chances of getting the wrong one. Yes, we can hook one perhaps, but a hook in him is a hook in us. We either end up neurotically obsessed, or he figures out it's a hook and does his own casting off. When we attract love by an intensified connection to the spirit inside, we take responsibility for the energy around us, harmonizing it in such a way that those who come forward—who we sense are meant to be with us— connect with us out of similarly pure intent.

Surrender of the partner obsession is a great release and allows much greater room for real love to enter. Be friends with a person. Don't underestimate the grace of true friendship. If passion is to follow, don't worry that it won't. But sex isn't everything; and until we know that, we are slaves to something stupid. And when we get that figured out, then everything, including sex, gets better.

Our entire life is a cycle of desire: desire satisfied, desire felt, desire satisfied and then felt again. Sex keeps rhythm. When we love a man, we love from the bottom of all souls, from our source, from the center of things, from God. If men only knew what a blessing our love is. And if we only knew what a blessing it is to be loved by them. To say "I love you" and to mean it is the same thing as saying "God bless you."

When he is not with us but we can feel him inside us anyway, when we can feel his energy penetrate our own, we long to squeeze him, as we do when making love. The electron microscope has revealed that when the sperm finally makes its way to the egg, the egg lifts itself up a bit to meet its partner. We long to do that, and one of the most difficult parts of retrieving the inner female is standing the wait until he gets here.

And what is the purpose of having an intimate partner? The purpose of intimacy is to massage the heart, to soften the muscles around our hardened places and keep pliant the places where we're already open. The circle of love is deep and strong. It can forgive mistakes and cast out error. It can foster greatness and bring forth new life. There is nothing it cannot do. Love is God.

It's no accident that millions of people say, "Oh, God," when they come. That's because he's there and they saw him. He *is* those moments when there is no argument, just pure connection. That *is* God. It's not *like* God, or *sort of* God, or to be thought about *in terms of* God. Love is God. To love another person— and I'm not saying that every time we come we love, but on the other hand it happens often enough to warrant the conversation—is to experience the divine.

Now isn't there something we should look at here? Isn't there a gigantic hippopotamus sitting on humanity's coffee table, outliving generations? Yet no one comments on its presence. Isn't there one creature who keeps nagging, cajoling, weeping, begging, and conniving—however functionally or dysfunctionally—for relationships that work? Aren't women the creatures who simply refuse to get off the subject?

Women keep talking about human connections because we are coded to do so. We came into the world with the memory in our soul that this is our function here. It is not our weakness, our neurosis, or our addiction. It is our strength. And when we are denied the power of a valid voice, it is not only we but the whole world that suffers.

There's a fossil in all our brains, the obsolete consciousness, the dominator, the tyrant, the unbalanced masculine, the mean one. It's not time to overthrow it because the woman in us doesn't overthrow. She doesn't have to. But it's time to ignore it, that voice of contempt for the humanistic stance. It's frightening but not dangerous—like a dead rat. It isn't some genius. It is anti-life and therefore stupid.

A BOYFRIEND ONCE said to me, "I had an erection today when I thought about you. You women have no idea what effect you have on guys."

That's true. We don't. And that's because we lie to each other constantly. Men pretend they don't care, and we pretend we don't care back. We are all liars. We do not stand naked. We make love but not always truthfully. We have become sluts and whores and barren of poetry.

Sex is a powerful spiritual identity. When we are in it, when we are truly in it, when we are making love and are crazed with desire, then we touch who we are and can rejoice in the knowledge. Now, stop the frame. Why can't we live there? Why shouldn't we live there? When we do not claim and nurture the experience of love, then the experience becomes unavailable to us.

Sex is not the ultimate high, but the ultimate high hangs out around sex. The ultimate high is the dance with another person, played so deep down and with such abandon that glee returns to grown-ups. Sex is not always noble, but love is noble, and people who love each other have sex. Their noble hearts make a good thing great.

Art is not the ultimate high, but the ultimate high is expressed in art. The ultimate high is a creative surge of inner knowing, bursting forth through personal constriction and given as a gift to the universe around us. Art is noble. It makes life higher. Sex and art together, that's good.

What else makes sense when all is reduced to what really matters? Reverence and worship and prayers for peace—they also matter. Everything else is peripheral, although interesting perhaps and fun at times.

What would the world be like if the guiding principle of our lives were this: We will do nothing, support nothing, conspire with nothing that could possibly hurt anyone? This cuts to essential knowledge, that we must stand up to protect the children no matter what, no matter where. And we are all children. Any commitment less than that, any goal but total harmlessness is a rejection of the Goddess. And what would happen if we all agreed—all of us, in some mass consortium— that this would be our creed? That we would return to what is pure in our hearts?

Sex would be better. Our art would be better. And I'll tell you what the world would be like. There would be no political, social, economic, or ecological problems, because their causes would have been removed. If harmlessness becomes the order of the day, problems will be replaced by the joy of creating joy. All we will do is pray, create, and make love—or some variations thereof, forever.

Pray for your loved one often: Dear God, bring him

happiness and peace. We want him present so we can touch his spirit from a closer place. We touch his eyes so we can take joy in the fact that he really exists. We want him to be happy so miracles can happen around him.

See him as you want him to be: in such deep peace, full of every feeling that would make him melt. If we can fully imagine one human being, completely happy, then we can begin to imagine heaven. And that is why we learn to love: to care so completely for one other person that our hearts break open wide and we learn to love them all. That's the meaning of love and the purpose of love, that one other person might signify our love for God and all humankind. It's a place where love is holy and sex is holy and the earth itself is reconceived.

SIX

A Golden Cord

Oh the mother and child reunion
Is only a motion away

—Paul Simon

What happens around a dinner table when a family gathers at early evening? What does a holiday meal mean? What feelings stay with a child forever when he or she is tucked into a sweet bed and read a bedtime story? The answer to all the above is "More than you know."

Human development is an invisible unfolding of energies and feelings that cannot be charted or boxed or reduced to formulas. It is sacred ground, the Goddess's territory. It has been trampled on and must be replanted. The fabric of our lives has been rent and must be rewoven. We must re-create the experience of home. This is a feminine function in both men and women. It does not have to be a woman who takes care of the home; a man can do the job as well. But we must all recognize how important it is that the work get done. "Out in the world" is not inherently a more important place for someone to be than inside the home. Inside the home, we become the people we are outside.

Too many people in our culture, rich and poor alike, do not have family or friends to come home to at night, do not have a home environment that is gentle, do not have someone who cares where they are or cares how they are feeling. We are falling apart inside, and that is why we are falling apart outside.

One of my favorite things in life is having picnics on my bed. Not necessarily picnics with food, but picnics with fun and talk and feelings and friends. I have a king-size bed, which I find a requisite for family life. And by family, I don't mean just my daughter and me. I mean a group experience of love and support.

Four people are on my bed as I write this. There's me, propped up on pillows with my laptop computer; Norma, sixty-five, who has worked with me since I started lecturing years ago; my daughter, two; Lisa, twenty-two, a student in fashion design who is helping me take care of her this weekend. Norma and Lisa are reading out loud from a giant copy of *The Three Little Pigs*.

We have just spent half an hour discussing whether or not we should be more forceful in getting the baby off her bottle. My mother thinks she's too old to still suck on a bottle, but then again that's from the woman who brought up at least one oral compulsive that I know of. A friend of mine, who is a teacher and knows about these things, told me to calm down. "Are you worried that she's going to walk up the aisle with a bottle in her mouth?" On another day, my sister, Jane, had suggested that we have a bottle-throwing-away ceremony, where my daughter would acknowledge that she's a big girl now, and we would ritualistically throw away all the bottles. I think she's too young for that. I decide to leave her alone and let her drop it when she drops it. I ask her if she would like to take a bath with Mommy, and she responds, "Maybe." I've never heard her use that word before, much less express such ambivalence about bathing with her mother.

I keep thinking that this scene is like a three-dimensional Mary Cassatt. What I love most about it is the communion of women and particularly our generational span. I'm sitting here thinking this is a beautiful, beautiful life I have, when I make the ridiculous decision to pick up the *Los Angeles Times*.

So this is what happened yesterday: A four-year-old black boy was sleeping in his bed when bullets started ripping through the walls from the apartment next door. Walls in tenement houses are as thin as paper. We have no way of knowing, of course, whether little Germaine had moments of terror before the bullets hit him, whether he sat up, whether he cried out. That's something neither we nor his mother will ever know. All we know is that bullets penetrated the wall, and in a matter of minutes this baby lay dead.

How does his mother live with this? How do I live with this? How do any of us live with this? I am in grief, confusion, despair, frustration, and total outrage. I blame drug dealers, Mafia bosses, bigoted politicians, gun manufacturers, NRA lobbyists, and Hollywood types who've pushed violence down our throats like syrup laced with strychnine for the last thirty years. And what I want to know is this: Why was that beautiful little white girl who fell down a well in Texas a few years ago so much more important than Germaine Johnson from East L.A.? Why is his life not more valuable to us? And why does Kuwait matter to us more than our own children?

What are we going to do about this? Simply work individually, within our own families, with our own children, to spread peace and love as deeply as we can? I'm not sure we can afford to be too slow about this. As Dante wrote in the *Inferno*, "The hottest place in hell is reserved for those who, in times of crisis, preferred to remain neutral." But what is the most empowered, the most spiritually perfect position to take? I don't know, but I utter a prayer.

I ask God for help. Let this darkness be cast away from earth. Show us how to make miracles happen. Deliver these children. Deliver us all. Do for us, God, what we can't do for ourselves. Heal our minds of violent thoughts, that violence might disappear from earth. Help us recover. Help us rise. We open our hearts to receive your guidance. We're ready to change. Amen.

I pick up my daughter and hold her in my arms. Thank you, God, for letting her be born into so much love and abundance. Let every baby be blessed and protected, not just my own, but every one. There are so many babies in this world who are sick, and no one cares for them; who are dirty, and no one changes their diapers; who are hungry, and no one feeds them. Shame on us all for doing so little. And God help us all, on the day when the shit finally hits the fan.

Children remind us of what's important. They help return us to a too-often lost perspective, where we stand in relation to generations before and after us. A woman I once met, herself a mother of four, told me that having children "gives us all the things we pray for, like respect and patience and understanding." I was impressed by the nature of her prayers.

We don't have to give birth to children to know we're the mothers of the world. We are the wombs of the generations that follow, not only physically but emotionally, psychologically, and spiritually. Our bodies are the space that prepares and sustains our children's physical life, and our personalities the space that prepares and sustains their emotional life. For better or for worse, within our being they form into who they are. We are all mothers to all children. Every woman everywhere, whether she works in an advertising agency, politics, or the entertainment industry; whether she teaches, sells, waits on tables, answers phones, or just wakes up in the morning, is part of our motherhood. We cannot protect our children from the collective mass of female vibrations, nor should we want to. The world is meant to be a safe and nurturing environment for children. The fact that it isn't is a sacred call to action for every conscious woman. In this way, we will heal our children and the children still living psychically within us.

ABORTION CAN BE an overwhelming loss. That doesn't mean it shouldn't be legal—I think it should—but that still doesn't mean it's not a terrible emotional pain. We have never come to terms with the fact that for the first time in our social history millions of women turned away their children. And we did do that. There is no pretending that we didn't. There are certain times when we think maybe we shouldn't have, times when we wish with anguish that we hadn't, and times when we have seen, and still see, no other way of proceeding. However we see it, guilt is not helpful. It is not a part of God's vision. No one is guilty, but lots of us are sad.

Don't get waylaid by politics or swayed by false religion. Stay close to your heart, where your feelings are honest and authentic and raw. Abortion is a bitch. Scream and yell at all you have lost, cry and mourn over what you are doing, but never pretend it's a casual thing. It is not. It is a mother saying good-bye to her child and a woman declining a miracle. Talk to

God. Talk only to God. Mourn your lost children. Pray for an easier world.

I HAVE FOUNDED charitable organizations, run them, and raised hundreds of thousands of dollars to support them. I have lectured around the world to many thousands of people, and I have written a number-one bestselling book. *Raising a child is harder.*

It takes more energy, more focus, more sensitivity, and if done well, at least as much intelligence. And if we raised happy children, we wouldn't *need* so many charities, lectures, and books on how to have a happier, more balanced life. The idea that a woman is somehow doing more with her life if she has a job out in the world is insane. There is no such thing as a nonworking mother. Having waited so long to have children, the baby boom generation can be blind to the incredible burden—however joyous it is—of bringing up children. This will change now as more and more people begin to realize there is no job in the world that, when done well, requires more work and intelligence than raising our sons and daughters.

Women will continue to be oppressed, socially and politically, until we recognize the roles traditionally associated with women as being among the most important in our society. Someone's got to take care of the house and raise the kids. The *I Ching* says that if the family unit is healthy, then society is healthy; and when the family falls apart, society falls apart. How

dare we make a woman feel that her life is less important if it is lived in service to family, children, and
home? And how dare we make a man feel that his life
is more important if it is not?

We are all here to serve each other, and the choice
to do that is no less valid when the people we serve
are the ones in our own family. During the recent
presidential election, Hillary Clinton was attacked for
having the audacity to be a strong woman with a mind
of her own. I understand her predicament very well.
But there's another side to the Hillary question. It's
great that she takes an active role politically, but one
of her most important functions as First Lady is to help
Bill Clinton emotionally, to provide him and their
daughter with the feminine, intimate, personal support that every person needs in order to live most
powerfully in the world. Every prospective First Lady
is now asked what she would do if she got the job.
Jacqueline Kennedy had said that her greatest service
to the nation while she lived in the White House
would be to take care of John Kennedy. There was a
time when I would have found that an unliberated
answer. Today, I find it sublime, sane, and feminist.

It is feminist because it honors the role of the feminine—nurturing, care giving, compassionate, loving—
whether it is performed by a man or a woman. How
do we quantify, for others to see, the energy it takes—
emotionally, intuitively, spiritually, intellectually,
physically—to love well? And no one is more important to love than the members of our own families.

The fact we have forgotten this over the past twenty-five years or so has left a trail of psychic blood in our culture that is no small wound, no small tragedy.

WHEN I MENTIONED to a friend that child raising is such hard work, she responded, "Exactly. That's why so many women are opting not to have children. They figure they can't do it and also have successful careers outside the house." To which I said, "Well, men don't have to make that choice. No one ever says about a man, 'I wonder whether he'll go for the career or have kids instead.' "

Neither should women have to think in terms of that choice. As society heals, children are invited into our lives in new and more wholesome ways. Big businesses often now include gyms in their buildings; a few years ago, this would have seemed ridiculous. So too, hopefully just ahead, businesses will include child care and even educational programs for children among their facilities. Not just for mothers, but for fathers as well. We don't just need mothers and all good women around our children; we also need fathers and all good men around them too.

Computers have revolutionized professional life, and more and more people now work out of their homes. I write books with my child playing on the bed next to me. What enables me to do this is excellent child care. Child care should be recognized for its tremendous importance. Were we to apply our dollars intelligently to the people who take care of children, we would spend millions of dollars less on the damage done to our society by wounded adults. Wounded children become wounded adults, and wounded adults can destroy the world.

A key to mothering is to visualize our children as the adults we would love them to become: strong, happy, serious, loving. Now imagine what kind of mother they must have had to grow into such fabulous grown-ups. And whatever that is, becoming it is the task that lies before us.

Most people are not great parents because they don't want to take the time to do the job well. It takes time to explain to a child the truthful, conscious answers to all his or her questions. It takes intuition and skill to track his or her thoughts and feelings. It takes more than most of us are willing to give to protect a child from the meaningless stimulus of the world around him or her. Yet there is no single effort more radical in its potential for saving the world than a transformation of the way we raise our children. They must grow up to be adults with only a fraction of our neuroses, or the world is in serious trouble. This is not the time to mimic our parents. It is a time to reverse the trend.

We can do it. I know we can. For we have had the time to think—and many of us have—about what we were not given and were not shown when we were children. And now with our own kids, we have the chance to rewrite history, to parent them as we wish we had been parented. And thus does our own reparenting occur. We release the past as we release the future.

Children are not children. They are just younger people. We have the same soul at sixty that we had at forty, and the same soul at twenty-five that we had when we were five. If anything, children are wiser. They know more than we do, and have at least as much to teach us as we have to teach them. How dare we try to fit them into our boxes and make them play by our rules, which are so very, very stupid? How dare we tell them anything when we live in a world so obviously backward? And how ungrateful and irreverent we are to listen so little and watch so casually when angels themselves have moved into the house.

I have never seen such honest demonstrations of enlightenment as in happy children. They laugh a lot, yet they are very serious. They understand everything without letting on that they understand much. They are old and young, innocent and loving. What are we doing pretending to know more than they do? And why are we putting the things of this world before their well-being? We tend to treat children as we treat God. Not always well.

Having a child has shown me, and continues to show me each passing day, the importance of listening. When we listen deeply to another person, we gain the power that comes from joining. Trying to put across our own idea or wish without first finding common emotional ground with the child or other adult will only bring out resistance, whether acted out now or later.

The most important thing I have learned about children is the need to show them respect and patience. We hear so much talk about children respecting their elders, and yet we see so many instances where they obviously don't. But how would they learn respect if they are not shown respect? Many people treat children as if they're not as smart as grown-ups. But there is a big difference between not being as smart and just not knowing the language yet.

Although great strides have been made in the fields of child psychology and development, every woman should remember that we have the intuitive radar to know exactly how to listen to our children, what to say to our children, and how to love our children. Parenting classes and books can be helpful, but their main purpose should be to serve as tools by which we are put in touch with our natural wisdom, not directed away from it. Good parenting is not intellectual as much as emotional and intuitive. There is a golden cord that ties a mother to her child. It is God's knowingness that is placed within us. There is no one who knows as well as we do what our children want and need. We learn what they want, we learn what they need, by listening to them and watching them. They know, and they will tell us.

Several years ago, I held a weekly gathering for mothers and small children, our conversation based on the spiritual principles I taught in my lectures on *A Course in Miracles*. Before our first meeting, I meditated and asked what I should say to the assembled mothers. What I felt in my meditation was this: it was not my job to teach these women about mothering but, rather, to remind them that the mother is the first and primary spiritual teacher. Women *know* what to do. The problem is our having been dissociated from our own essential knowledge. My only purpose was to remind the women that motherly wisdom flows through them as naturally as mother's milk. Our love is a form of mother's milk.

Mothers are spiritual teachers. We teach love to our children by showing them respect and patience and tenderness. They will learn to give love in the ways they receive it from us and see us give it to others. It is not enough for us to know that we love our children. We must ask ourselves very seriously what this means.

Part of loving is helping people find their own strength. Dorothy Canfield Fisher said, "A mother is not a person to lean on, but a person to make leaning unnecessary." Our children are not extensions of ourselves. We did not create them; God did. We are here to supervise their development, not dictate their reality. They are their own beings. We must not seek to impose our own rhythms on them, but, rather, help them find and maintain their own. We can be the space in which a child's way of being is so respected that he or she finds a greater inner ease. That is the priestly function of motherhood.

I can see on my daughter's face when she is being denied her right to express who she is. There are times when her desires would deny those of others, of course, and it is my job to teach her that other people are as important as she is. But children can be taught that. I tell my child, "You can have whatever you want, darling, unless it is dangerous or it lacks integrity or it would make you a spoiled brat." Of course, she doesn't yet know what all those words mean, but I'm telling you, she gets the gist. I don't understand why people talk to their kids as if they were idiots and then plan to spring deeper truths on them at some later date. And who is then going to talk to them about things that matter? Teachers at school? Can we count on that? It is our job.

A friend once said to me that it's important to say yes to a child whenever possible, instead of no. Instead of pointing out what they can't do, we can point out all the things they can do. We want to teach children about ever-increasing possibilities, not ever-decreasing ones. All of these things become, after all, the mental habits they will carry with them all their lives.

Look at what we've been doing to our children. Starting with parents and then our educational system, we have taught children repeatedly that they are not the power centers of their own lives. We train them into a kind of slavery, by teaching them the ways of those who let other people determine what their lives will be, what their options will be, and how they can serve a system outside themselves. We live in a society where a small percentage of people call the shots: A vast majority serve a social or business structure centered outside themselves that cares not one bit for their hearts or their souls. Our educational system promotes this, training children to be perfect cogs in the wheel that keeps our system rolling. Although we enjoy extensive political freedom in this country, most of us have severely limited emotional and psychological freedom. They have been all but capped by the time we are five years old, by so many voices telling us what we can and cannot do. What good is having freedom when we don't know how to access it, how to give ourselves permission to use it?

Respect for authority does matter. But as important as it is to defer to the boss, it is equally important to make the boss the boss and no one else. Our government, for instance, is not our boss. We are its boss. Big distinction, and one too easily forgotten by disempowered people.

Some parents teach children, "The world is yours. Go out there and get it. Enjoy yourselves!" Other children are taught that the world is a tough place where it's hard to find abundance. Children soak up these messages like dry sponges, and they stand in line, with everyone else who has been told by their parents what reality is, to live the lives prescribed for them at a young and tender age.

The economic problems in this country do not stem from financial breakdown, but from a breakdown of hope and enthusiasm. How can you be enthusiastic when you don't believe there is anything out there for you, when it seems that others have all the power and get all the breaks? We must teach our children that the abundance in the world is infinite and available to everyone because it comes from within us. As we teach our kids to bless the world, celebrate the world, and embrace the world, we hand them the keys to success.

As mothers and fathers, we must teach children not only to think for themselves but also to make decisions for themselves. Otherwise, they will grow up to be adults with little or no capability to make intelligent decisions for their own lives much less for their society and their planet. And whether we like it or not, we are living at a momentous time on earth when our capacity to find the best within ourselves and live from that place and change the world accordingly may possibly determine whether or not we survive.

What could be more important for the future of our world than that we raise happy and well-adjusted, empowered and empowering children? They are the caretakers of tomorrow's world, and they will be ready for the job or not. This is not just a woman's issue; it is the issue most central to our society's healing and growth. Every woman and every man too, must take responsibility in their hearts for all children. As the parental generation, every child is our child. To ignore the state of our children is to ignore the state of our world.

• • •

OUR RELATIONSHIPS ARE POISONED by the failure of both men and women to realize that in each of us a lion roars. We do not yet recognize that the fierceness of the lioness is as right and beautiful as the roar of the lion. Humans are the only species in which the female is made wrong for showing she is pissed.

The mother of any species is loving and tender toward her young but fiercely protective whenever they are threatened. What has happened to the female of our species? Do we not see the dangers that hover? Are we under the impression that our children and our children's children can survive the ecological and social and spiritual breakdown stalking our planet? Our young are threatened. Children are dying. This is not the time to spend all day primping.

Keep a vigil. Stay awake in the garden. Hold to the light. Revere goodness and integrity and truth. And most of all, let us teach these things to our children. We must counter the horrors of a world that doesn't care: a system that spews darkness, media that spew violence, governments that spew apathy, and industries that spew poison.

If the relationship between mothers and children is returned once again to the relationship God intends it to be—between a soul new to earth and its primary spiritual teacher here—then children will grow up to know that neither money nor fame nor prestige nor power is nearly as important as a life lived for noble purpose. And there is no greater nobility than to live with compassion for all living things and to eschew,

with every ounce of our being, the forces of fear that run goodness into the ground at every possible turn.

Fear is hard-heartedness in all its forms. Sometimes it is disguised in quasi-religious clothes, seeking to judge whom God would have us love. Sometimes it hides behind our right to free expression, smugly justifying the violence that bombards us in movies and television. But although it hides, it cannot be hidden. It is always knowable by its absence of heart. It does not promote life. It does not protect children. It does not love.

Women must remember the sacred nature of our Goddess self, the call to glory inherent in human incarnation. We are daughters of history and mothers to a new world. This is not the time to throw away our power. It is time to claim it, in the name of love.

SEVEN

The Castle Walls

One is not born, but rather becomes, a woman.
—Simone de Beauvoir

Electing women to positions of political power does not in itself guarantee the expression of a feminine voice in the external world. Once in power, women can be tempted to conspire with the paternalistic system that they feel has so magnanimously allowed them a place at the table. They feel compelled to be strong men among strong men. Only when women go into the world to express an authentic balance of intelligence with compassion, representing not only women but the effort within all human beings to retrieve our lost hearts, will there be genuine liberation of the imprisoned Goddess.

And what is the imprisoned Goddess? Our contempt for passion, our invalidation of feminine, non-linear modes of thinking and being, our repudiation of feeling, our rolled eyes at the suggestion that love is indeed the answer. And who holds her prisoner? Women and men alike. During the Clarence Thomas confirmation hearings, many women uttered about men, "They just don't get it." And one reason they so often don't get it is that we ourselves so often don't.

Every time a woman at a dinner party fails to support another woman who dares to express herself with pure emotion and power, she is betraying the Goddess. And why? Don't miss this, girls. Because at the deepest levels, we're afraid we won't be attractive to the men at the table if we dare to voice our hearts. We're afraid we won't be as sexy as we would be if we just sat there and played china doll, making no waves, threatening no man.

Thus we betray one another. We break the covenant of sisters. All this, I think, because we're so afraid of losing Daddy. We lost him once, and the pain is too terrible to endure again. Daddy wasn't there or didn't think our feelings mattered, so why should anyone else? And if we don't matter, we cannot be loved. Our thoughts matter, perhaps, if they mimic his, but anything too emotional is crossing the line.

But there are men in the world who are healthier than Daddy was, who think your feelings are beautiful and applaud your passion. The men at the table are not Daddy, and the ones who are, are not your men. There are new men appearing now, just as there are new women. And they will not only accept your voice, they will squeeze your hand under the table and silently urge you to continue.

"But where are they?" you ask. You would love to meet a man like that, but you never do. If such men are not yet in your life, it is because they are not yet magnetized to you. There is nothing in your energy now to suggest to them that they are honored here. The healthiest men are magnetized to the healthiest women.

Or you might be thinking, "I wish my husband or boyfriend were like that." Here is a magical secret we all need to know: People change. No one is stuck who chooses not to be. No one is without infinite potential for a radical turnaround—from all that is unconscious and fearful and weak to all that is conscious and loving and strong. Never think you know someone inside and out, because unless your knowingness includes all the possibilities for magnificence that lie latent within that person, you know relatively little. In a way, only God knows any of us.

It is a woman's function to mother the world by holding the idea of its possible perfection within her heart. We give birth to children, to men, to businesses, to each other. It is not the uterus but the heart that is our real womb. What emerges from the heart is a co-creation with God. To give birth to a child is not an inherently conscious act. To produce a happy child, as a parent, a teacher, a friend, or a society, is to successfully fulfill a divine function. Mary holding the

Christ child is not a trillion paintings for nothing.

Our question must be this: What do we want to give birth to? The feminine self within both men and women is waiting for conscious impregnation. The Goddess has been raped when she should have been honored. She has been abused when she should have been worshiped. She has been patient when she could have been cutting. But something has changed.

She will give birth to herself through all of us, and our only choice is whether she shall emerge with fury or show up sweet and friendly. She's here. There's no holding her back. But what she will look like is up to each and every woman and, to some extent, each and every man. This, to me, is the meaning of women's liberation: that the woman within us and the women around us might be liberated from the grotesque and degrading thought system that still pervades our earth, viewing the feminine as weak or unworthy, unnecessary to hear or unimportant to love.

I HAVE A COUPLE OF GIRLFRIENDS who were recently fired from their jobs. They were both upset, understandably, but in both cases I felt as though they had been given the boot—what Barbara De Angelis has described as the aggressive action of the universe when we have refused to take the steps we know in our hearts are right for us to take next. I had heard both women say numerous times, "I've got to get out of this business." But they hadn't, because life seemed to have placed them where they were, and from a rational, ego-driven perspective they couldn't see their way out.

My friends are examples of a current phenomenon among women: women who are here to tell the truth, raise the spiritual rafters, blow the roof off the paradigm that has ruled and oppressed us for the last few thousand years. They're wearing the mask of Modern American Woman, but that's not all they were born for, and on some level they know it. Without a conscious conception of the spiritual meaning and purpose of our lives and its relationship to our everyday careers, we live stymied by our own circumstances whether we are successful in a worldly sense or not.

We are spiritual healers dressed in worldly drag. We keep trying to find a masculine niche for our feminine powers, but I'm not sure why. We must lead with the power of our womanly knowingness and let new careers take shape around it. First, we must make a commitment in our hearts to healing the world; we must embrace the understanding that we were born as women to do this. This understanding releases a power that breaks through all confusion and lower energies of the world, to create for us the circumstances that support us in our higher task.

Many women I know are already living attuned to their feminine radar while fully involved in worldly careers. They are forging new paths of feminine participation in the worldly dance. They know the ultimate purpose of their careers, which is the same as the purpose of our bodies and our relationships: to do the

Goddess's work, to do what we can to give birth to a new world. It ultimately doesn't matter whether we start a company, nurse a child, produce a movie, or make a soup. What really matters is that we do it with love.

THE LOVE WE SHOW must extend to one another. When my first book was published, I appeared as a guest on Oprah Winfrey's television show. As we sat in front of the cameras, I heard Oprah praise my book and tell the audience that she herself had bought a thousand copies. From that point on, it became a bestseller. Due to Oprah's generosity and enthusiasm that day, my professional life took a giant leap forward.

While it is true that Oprah has tremendous power and influence, I realized upon reflection that every woman can be an Oprah to someone. Imagine what the world would be like if every woman showed support to at least one other woman, standing behind her in some way on the ladder of success. Oprah seems to have the desire to share with others what she has received, and I would imagine this consciousness is part of her huge success. What she demonstrated to me was the power of sisterhood, where a woman helps another woman and others are helped in the process.

We must not fail to learn from the lessons of women who share their bounty of opportunity and influence and power and goodwill. There is a mountaintop with enough room for all of us. None of us will get there and stay there unless all of us get there and stay there. If women succeed only in isolated cases, the professional world will continue to be unsure ground for women in general. We must take the communion of women very seriously at this time and do all we can do to support other women in reaching for the stars. There cannot be too many glorious women. There cannot be too many queens. There cannot be too much success.

There's a lot of talk today about whether a woman can have it all. The problem isn't having it all but receiving it all, giving ourselves permission to have a full and passionate life when our cultural conditioning has denied us that for centuries. The biggest limit to our having is our small reach, our shy embrace. As long as it's considered unfeminine to have a full appetite— which it is, because it is recognized that whatever we allow ourselves to truly desire we usually get—then we will not sit down at life's banquet but only at its diner. This is ridiculous, and it holds back the entire world for women to live at half-measure. It's also an insult to men to suggest that they can't dance with goddesses, as though a woman at full power might step on their toes.

For some men, perhaps, a glorious woman is too much of a threat, but not for all of them. Men are changing just as we are, and together we are widening the path of emotional opportunity for women. This is our biggest block to power: the embarrassed looks when we express ourselves, the feeling in the room that we've gone too far whenever we've pushed any envelopes that matter. Men have got to realize—and so have we—that something of ancient significance is rising up from the bottom of things and spilling out through all of us. Men feel it; women feel it. Women, however, are going crazy around it because our nervous systems are tied to its expression. It's a pregnancy we can't abort; and when we try to, we get even crazier than we were. We might as well accept the fact that nature is turning the world on its ear, and she's chosen us to announce the news.

WHEN I WAS in my early twenties, I went with a date to a nightclub in New York. Appearing there were two talented young musicians, Daryl Hall and John Oates. Although we would later know them as Hall and Oates, at that time they were known but not that well known, and their music had the fabulous impact of fresh beginnings and new sounds.

Something happened to me that night. I had been to many concerts before, but I had never experienced as I did then the transcendent way a musician can bring an entire room into a single heartbeat. I remember thinking, "They're priests; that's what they really are. They're priests." They weren't taking me on a magic-carpet ride to music. Music was the magic carpet on which they were taking me somewhere else, that somewhere else the land and sky inside ourselves. It's the purpose of our lives to find that place and stay in it.

After that, I grew more in love with music and live performance but, most important, I became enthralled with the idea that a human being could create a space, through music or anything else, where peoples' hearts are harmonized and lifted up. I knew that was what music did, and literature and philosophy and all art. What fascinated me was not just the role of art but the role of the artist, not just philosophy but the role of the philosopher. What gave a person the magician's wand, that he or she could wield such awesome power and transport whole groups of people to an enchanted land?

And that's what I wanted to be when I grew up. I wanted to take people higher, the way artists did, and philosophers. I fell in love with the thought that a human life could be a priestly conduit, a connecting link between earth and sky. It didn't matter, then, whether we were artists, philosophers, teachers, or rabbis. What mattered was that we laid down our ego lives, that we might be used as some sort of highway to a life that lay beyond all this. And as I grew and as I stumbled and, most important, as I began to love and be loved, I realized that the ultimate priest is the lover inside us, and the ultimate priesthood is the role of friend and loved one.

The issue is not just to bring groups of people into higher realms through art or philosophy or politics or religion but to find a way to bring those close to us into that space, through the energies of our lives. The role of friend, then, is a priestly function, as is the role of lover, wife, husband, and parent. In the priestly role, we hold a space within us for the splendor of life and the splendor of people. And then, when we are present, the people around us can see more clearly what is possible for them and possible for all of us. We become miracle workers and healers as we take on the mantle of a serious humanness. The earth is lifted past the dark and heavy, dense and tragic energies that pervade it still, to the clearer, sweeter air of the land in the sky. A child is comforted when Mommy and Daddy are present. Let all the world feel comfort now. God and Goddess are back together.

SEVERAL YEARS AGO I started working out at a health club in Los Angeles. Soon after I began, I became aware of a man who spent a lot of time in the gym, was liked by most everyone, but had an exaggerated way of flirting with every woman there. Most women played along, allowing him to kiss them and make sexual innuendos every time he saw them, but it also seemed to me that none of them liked it. No one told him to buzz off, but I couldn't help feeling that a lot of women wanted to. His behavior was disrespectful and exploitative. I knew I was going to have a problem because it was just a matter of time before he got around to me.

He was obviously in some ways a very nice person, and I knew it wouldn't go down very well for me to make some comment about sexual harassment or male chauvinist behavior. I also knew by this time that defense and attack are low-level approaches to life's problems. I remember saying a prayer as I walked downstairs to the gym one day, asking God to give me a miracle. I couldn't figure out a way of dealing with this, so I was praying for some kind of inspired solution.

As I walked across the room to the Nautilus machines, there he was. I went right up to him, put out my hand to shake his, and said, "Hi! I'm Marianne Williamson. It's so nice to meet you." He shook my hand and introduced himself, meeting me emotionally on exactly the same level of dignity with which I had approached him. It was amazing to me how respectfully he behaved toward me after that. I had been proactive in my approach to him, not waiting for him to harass me before figuring out how to react, but going to him with the highest level of behavior I could in an effort to remind him of my honor and his as well.

We have great power to affect the attitudes and behavior of the people around us, at work and at home. We have the power to set a tone of honor, to create an energy around ourselves that says, "I respect myself. I respect you. Let's respect each other." Often we compromise that energy because we want to appear sexy more than we want to appear serious. But we pay for that, and so do the women around us. There are men who harass women no matter what we do. For those men who still stand at the crossroads and are trying to figure things out themselves, there's a lot we can do to support them in taking the higher road.

• • •

WHEN AMERICAN SETTLERS moved into the Wild West, shootings occurred regularly up and down the streets of new towns. Once women joined up with the men, however, things changed. The women said, "Stop it, you guys. No more shooting. The kids are here." And that was it. That's how civilization came to a theretofore uncivilized world.

And so it is that here, today, women can summon our internal powers, and as part of a mystical sisterhood, commit to ourselves that we shall no longer stand for the gratuitous sex and violence on our streets, in our movies, on television, or anywhere else. How badly we misuse our First Amendment right to freedom of speech when we use it to justify the grossest pollution of our psychic environment.

Do I think there should be censorship of any kind? Absolutely not. Do I think we all need to take more individual responsibility for the healing of the world? Absolutely, yes. There is a knee-jerk tendency to yell "First Amendment!" whenever anyone criticizes the media today. When someone yells out "First Amendment!" I yell back "Motherhood!" What about the rights of mothers and fathers? Shouldn't parents today be able to turn on the television, walk into the kitchen for five minutes, and know the chances are pretty good that our children won't witness a murder or two while we're tossing the salad? Shouldn't the minds of children be as important as the rights of huge conglomerates to make more and more millions of dollars?

I'm not talking about violence when it's a legitimate artistic or intellectual expression, as in movies like *Dances with Wolves*, *The Killing Fields*, *The Mission*, and many more. I'm talking about gratuitous sex and violence splattered all over American movies and television programs for no other reason—and I mean no other reason—than to sell tickets and to sell products. We are poisoning our children's spirits, and our own, for the sake of a dollar.

It is women who must make these matters an important issue today, simply because men aren't doing it. It's not that it's a woman's issue. It is a human issue, but it is being whispered about when it needs to be shouted about. And that is woman's work: to be the conscience of a society, to bring human issues to the forefront when some of our men friends and girlfriends have forgotten that violence always leads to death. Whether it's violence on TV, violence toward women, or violence in any other form, women have more power than we think to put our feet down and smash the dirt beneath our soles.

And there's a difference between erotica and pornography. Erotica celebrates women and sexuality. Pornography violates women and demeans sex. Since most pornography is the psychic rape of women, not men, then it must be women who collectively turn the tide back. As long as we're magicians now, let's get familiar with an important magical principle: turning things back.

It is as though the devil has gotten out of his box

and broken through some cracks in the walls that in a more perfect world would keep him ever at bay. But through the power of love, he can be turned back. To say, "In the name of God, Satan, get thee behind me!" means "Through the power of all that is beautiful in human beings, let all that is ugly go back to where it came from." And what you have to do after you say that is truly, truly mean it.

THERE IS A DIFFERENCE between obsession and passion. One form of emotional oppression of women is the cheap and automatic labeling of passionate emotion as obsession, something neurotic and wrong.

If an artist like Aretha Franklin sings about love from the bottom of her gut, we call it genius. If an ordinary woman talks about love from the bottom of her gut, we call it co-dependent, obsessed, or over-wrought. This leads women to distrust our own instincts, to think of our own passions as delusional or, at the very least, unladylike.

There's a difference between what a patriarchal thought system calls unladylike and what is unwomanly. When a woman gives birth to a child, she screams like a banshee. Screaming this way is certainly unladylike, but it is as womanly as things get. In years past and in some cases still today, men stayed away from the delivery room. The man remained outside the room while his partner gave birth to *their* child. He was not present for her pain, her physical genius, her creativity, or God's greatest miracle. How interesting.

Today in many places, things are different. A man tries to be present for the experience of a woman giving birth. He breathes through labor with her, as friend and partner. He doesn't leave the room; he holds her hand. What a shift this represents, from "I don't want to know" to "I don't want to miss this."

And what about a woman's corresponding labor, as she gives birth to other things, to the rest of her life? Birth is violent, whether it be the birth of a child or the birth of an idea. Beginning stages are rough. The most giant tree begins as a tiny green sprout, but that sprout pushes dirt out of its way as it forces itself up through the earth to the sunlight.

Should Michelangelo have always been calm, with so much talent and passion bursting through him? Or Georgia O'Keeffe, or Saint Teresa? We often find a common theme in biographies of talented people: In contrast to the brilliance of their art, their personalities were violent and their lives turbulent. The forces called violent and turbulent here were not *in contrast* to their brilliance; they were deeply felt, totally natural effects of a passionately lived life. How quickly we label the show of emotion as negative, particularly in women. How quick we are to label a woman's passion ugly, over the top, too much.

In a speech she gave recently in Hollywood, Barbra

Streisand claimed, "Language gives us an insight into the way women are viewed in a male-dominated society. A man shows leadership; a woman is controlling. If a man wants to get it right, he's looked up to and respected. If a woman wants to get it right, she's difficult and demanding." It is not just movie actresses who have a struggle on their hands when they have the audacity to buck the patriarchal system; it is any woman who dares to paint with all the colors on her emotional palette.

Women have more power than we know. When we truly understand the game for what it is and deepen our awareness of the most dangerous forms of female oppression—emotional and psychological— then we will be on our way to genuine liberation. It doesn't help to blame anyone. What we can do is face the truth. And any truth faced is closer to realization. True change doesn't emerge just from action; it emerges from genuine understanding. Action that stems from shallow understanding turns out to be shallow action. Action that flows from deeply felt consciousness is action that can change the world.

The Romanian dictator Ceauşescu argued that armies and weapons were not necessary to keep a people down as long as they are kept scared enough. And this is how women are oppressed in our society. We are afraid to allow ourselves to blossom fully because of the general disapproval that still fills the air whenever a "little lady" forgets her place.

But the more of us who understand the game and

see through the lie and forge ahead in support of every other woman's right to a passionate response to life, the more we will hasten the end of our jail term. Women have been imprisoned for ages, and in our cells, in our hearts, we have carried our true feelings like sleeping children, our spiritual issuance, our love. The prison walls are melting. We're almost out. And when we fly free, we will carry with us such gifts to the outside world. Our gifts haven't atrophied; they have grown in power. They have been waiting for centuries, and so have we.

Let's keep our eyes on the sky. They'll throw tomatoes; they'll lie about us and try to discredit us. But when they do, we'll remember the truth and bless our enemies and find strength in God. The regime of oppression is almost over; its life force is waning, and only its ghost remains. Don't tarry too long to mourn its effects; celebrate and rejoice in the new. The past is over. Wipe the dirt off your feet.

AFTER TAKING A WALK through the countryside one day, a painter friend observed to me that every flower has a different color deep down near its base, a color the flower doesn't show to the world. "Just like a woman," I said. "So do we."

Deep down, the woman inside us is different from the one we show in the light of day. She is more authentically sexual, more glamorous, more glowing, and she knows more. She tends to wait for her beloved to coax her out of her shell, but this wouldn't be true if the world showed her greater respect. She is afraid of being laughed at except when she is clearly desired. The whole world desires her actually, but doesn't usually let her know.

A woman I know wears a thin gold chain around her waist, under her clothes, with a charm bearing the inscription *Priceless*. It drives men crazy, she tells me. Small wonder. They love to be reminded of what they already know, since we live in a world that constantly denies it. She wears the chain, she says, in such a way that the charm falls perfectly across a certain female chakra, as it were, which reminds her constantly of her inestimable value.

So I say to myself, What would it take for us to remember our worth? How good we are, and how complete and loving and lovable. Men shouldn't have to bear the burden of our remembrance. It's not their function to remind us we are goddesses. It's our function to remember it and then reveal it to the world. When we remember, they will too. The light will be dazzling.

There is endless talk today about the role of women in our society. But we cannot have a meaningful discussion of our role without first establishing who we are at our core. Who a woman *is* must be determined before we can know what she is supposed to *do*. And when we are clear about that color at our base, our hidden identity, then what we show in the light of day will take on new power as well as new beauty.

Then, and only then, do we begin to understand

politics. As long as we focus on the outer world, which is not our home base, and try to wield power of the kind only known there (power so crude, by the way, the angels can't help but laugh), we will remain in the weaker, more slightly confused position.

When we remember we are queens from another kingdom, then the kings in this one will wake up at last and honor our presence and open the gates. We won't storm the castle walls; we will melt the castle walls. Kings will then set a table for us to feast at instead of tossing us bones. They will recognize us when we recognize ourselves. We come bearing gifts from another realm. We bring illumination when our minds are illumined. We are only visiting here, but our visit is an honor, a mitzvah, and the entire earth kingdom is blessed by our presence. Wake up and thank the stars. We have been playing so small and the crown is so huge. We will not wear it until we expand our heads.

Do you get it? Can you see? As we change our minds, we will change the world. And until we do, we will remain where we are. And all the laws and all the bashing and all the silly, childish, petty political arguments will continue for years, and for more years beyond, until women remember, followed by men, that a woman is a miracle and in her heart lies God. She is here to love God, passionately and truly, and to reveal to all others—men, children, and other women—that God is good and God is here. But we must be good, and we must be here, or our function is denied and the mission is aborted.

It's time to get started. It's time to wake up. Don't wait another minute. Claim your heart, and claim your glory. You have all you need. Bless other women. Do not tear them down. Remember they are you—your sisters, teachers, mothers, daughters. And then look on men with the new eyes the Goddess gives you, and then hold on. The new world will seem like nothing you have seen before. It will be reborn like you. It will shine like you. It will smile like you. It will feel like home.

At a certain point, our bitterness falls away, not in some epiphanic instant, but over countless years. It is the most joyous thing to feel ourselves aging backward, becoming more like children after having been like old women and it getting us nowhere. The sentence that used to bring hurt and pain and constriction to our faces then brings a childlike smile and a playful gaze.

Spiritual growth is like childbirth. You dilate, then you contract. You dilate, then you contract again. As painful as it all feels, it's the necessary rhythm for reaching the ultimate goal of total openness. The pain of childbirth is more bearable as we realize where it's leading. Giving birth to our selves, our new selves, our real selves, whether we are men or women, is a lot like giving birth to a child. It's an idea that is conceived, then incubates. Childbirth is difficult, but holding the child makes the pain worthwhile. And so it is when we finally have a glimpse of our own completion as human beings—regardless of our husband or lack of one, our boyfriend or lack of one, our job or lack of one, our money or lack of it, our children or lack of any, or whatever else we think we need in order to thrive and be happy. When we have finally touched on a spiritual high that is real and enduring, then we know that the pain of getting there was worth it, and the years ahead will never be as lonely.

God is father, and God is mother also. God has those two faces and a million more. Father God creates, protects, teaches, and empowers us. Mother God is the cosmic nurturer: she feeds us, cares for us, and holds us in her arms. Let's not argue over petty issues. God is both male and female, Father and Mother. And so are we. Beyond our gender, we are all just light. We are one with God, with each other and ourselves. Sex falls away that we might find union of a higher order. Any other knowledge is peripheral vision and ultimately blindness. The last thing to trip up on is whether God is male or female. Call it either; call it both. All that matters is that we call it, period.

And when we do, our hearts do melt. Our rage transmutes. Our burdens are released. And that is our birth into who we really are. It's messy and painful and noisy and big. But it's all that matters and it's all we're here for, to chuck these stupid clothes we wear, of false ambition and pride and fear, and come out naked and beautiful and new. And then it doesn't matter how old we are. We're young, we're old, we're neither, we're both. Every age bears a beautiful gift, its own brand of joy and loneliness and grief.

Let's become more beautiful with age, attaining the stature of the Jungian crone. Let's be wise and mature and queenly. Let's allow our centers of power to shift with grace, from focus on physical expression to focus on spiritual strength. The game isn't cruel except when played by the negative mind. In the life God has in mind for us, we grow more and more beautiful and know more and more joy. The longer we live, the more time we have to pursue the things that make life meaningful. Above all, let's not be ashamed of age. How often I've heard it said about a woman, "She's fifty. I'm telling you, she's not a day under," as though she had been caught in some crime. Youth is not a great prize, and age a sad afterthought. If anything, youth is the bud, and age is when we blossom.

Honor older women. Give them hope and support and sustenance. And allow them to pour out their gifts to you. What gifts they have. And when that happens, we youth instead of age. The older we get, the more we shed meaningless things and negative preoccupations. We become not harder with age but softer, not more bitter but more gentle. As we do, we will recognize that we are doing in fact what we came to earth to do. We are becoming the women we have wanted to be.

• • •

AND THAT IS THE STORY, the end of my tale. It's all I know, or at least all I have the power to write, of the journey in me and in every woman I've known.

I feel there's a depth to who we are and what we long for, so uncharted, so unmined, like a field of diamonds beneath the earth's surface. And in that field, we all lie latent. But there is arising around us, a shining through the rocks, and we are beginning to see and know and share its light. The world will be different for our daughters and sons because of our tears, our bravery, and our breakthroughs. One thing I know about all of us: We have tried so hard, and we are trying still. We are not without strength, and we are not without hope. We're trying our best to wear that crown. We have been imprisoned but we are now sprung free.

We still cry at times, but we're laughing too. There's a deep down belly laugh we've laughed only rarely, in the arms of someone beautiful who loved us and held on. We hold its memory close to our hearts and live for the day when we laugh that way again. We are about to break free. We are about to be born. We have seen the shining. We have seen. We have seen.

ACKNOWLEDGMENTS

My thanks to many people.

I thank Al Lowman, my agent, for his constant nurturing of the things it takes to keep me writing.

I thank Helen Morris at Random House for being the editor from heaven.

I thank Andrea Cagan for outstanding help as both editor and friend.

I thank Richard Cooper, who seems to understand everything.

I thank Harry Evans and all members of the Random House family.

And most of all, I thank the women who have gone deep with me and the men I have loved.